You
Wit

Praise for *Faerie Knitting*

"A beautiful book that takes flight
and transports knitting to a magical place.
I was enchanted by it all."

—NICKY EPSTEIN,
knitwear designer and author of *Nicky Epstein's Knitted Flowers*;
Knitting on the Edge; *Knitting Over the Edge*; and *Knitting Beyond the Edge*

"Through these new fairy tales that cleverly combine
knitting and storytelling, we return to the traditions of old,
where protagonists are innocent, good triumphs over evil, love
conquers all, and each knitted piece is transformative."

—SHIRLEY PADEN,
knitwear designer and author of *Knitwear Design Workshop*

"*Faerie Knitting* celebrates how stories and
knitting can work their magic and save our lives.
From the first page, I was enchanted."

—ANN HOOD,
author of *The Knitting Circle* and editor of *Knitting Yarns* and *Knitting Pearls*

Faerie Knitting

From the Bestselling Author of *Practical Magic* and *The Rules of Magic*

Faerie Knitting

ᴄᴡ 14 TALES OF LOVE AND MAGIC ᴄᴡ

FEATURES 14 ORIGINAL PATTERNS
Inspired by Each Story

ALICE HOFFMAN & LISA HOFFMAN

Adams Media
New York   London   Toronto   Sydney   New Delhi

Aadamsmedia

Adams Media
An Imprint of Simon & Schuster, Inc.
57 Littlefield Street
Avon, Massachusetts 02322

First Adams Media hardcover edition September 2018

ADAMS MEDIA and colophon are trademarks of Simon & Schuster.

For information about special discounts for bulk purchases, please contact Simon & Schuster Special Sales at 1-866-506-1949 or business@simonandschuster.com.

The Simon & Schuster Speakers Bureau can bring authors to your live event. For more information or to book an event contact the Simon & Schuster Speakers Bureau at 1-866-248-3049 or visit our website at www.simonspeakers.com.

Cover and interior design by Frank Rivera and Stephanie Hannus
Photography by Steve Parke
Additional images © Getty Images and 123RF

Manufactured in the United States of America

10 9 8 7 6 5 4 3 2 1

Library of Congress Cataloging-in-Publication Data
Hoffman, Lisa (knitwear designer), author. | Hoffman, Alice, author.
Faerie knitting / Alice Hoffman and Lisa Hoffman.
Avon, Massachusetts: Adams Media, 2018.
LCCN 2018011466 (print) | LCCN 2018016060 (ebook) |
ISBN 9781507206553 (hc) | ISBN 9781507206560 (ebook)
Subjects: LCSH: Knitting--Patterns. | Fairy tales--United States. | BISAC: CRAFTS & HOBBIES / Needlework / Knitting. | CRAFTS & HOBBIES / Fashion. | CRAFTS & HOBBIES / Needlework / Lace & Tatting.
Classification: LCC TT825 (ebook) | LCC TT825 .F34 2018 (print) | DDC 746.43/2041--dc23
LC record available at https://lccn.loc.gov/2018011466

ISBN 978-1-5072-0655-3
ISBN 978-1-5072-0656-0 (ebook)

DEDICATION

*With many thanks to my grandmother, Lillie, who told me my first fairy tales,
and to Lisa, my dear cousin, with gratitude for her artistry and friendship.*

—Alice

*To my children, Aaron, Ethan, Erica, and Nicholas,
and granddaughter, Reagan, my shining stars.
To my husband, Andrew, for your love and laughter.
And to my cousin, Alice, for being the best of both family and friend.*

—Lisa

The authors wish to thank Carolyn Turgeon
and *Faerie Magazine* for support and friendship.

CONTENTS

Story Introduction

Alice Hoffman

Fairy tales are the original stories passed down from grandmother to granddaughter on cold winter nights, when snow is falling and the fireplace is lit, when wolves lurk outside and the moon is bright. These are the tales that have lasted for centuries, continuing to have meaning for countless generations, stories that teach us about both the imagined and the real world as they warn us away from dark paths and dangerous beasts. Fairy tales bring us the deepest psychological truths. Even as children we can see past the fictional world of queens and castles and curses into our own modern lives. Truth is truth, no matter where a tale is set, in a forest or on the street where we live, and fairy tale themes provide a way for us to understand the complex web of relationships we are all bound to face. Who can you trust? Who is loyal and fearless? Who can rescue you better than you yourself can? Who can spin gold out of straw?

Fairy tales were the first stories I read, and they were also the very first stories I was told by my Russian grandmother. Her wondrous chronicles of a town where there was always snow and the river froze all year long, where wolves howled as she broke the ice to fetch water for her family each morning, were riveting. In each there was a lesson about bravery and self-reliance. *Always look over your shoulder when walking through the dark,* my grandmother told me. *Trust yourself most of all.*

Such stories are in the oral tradition of women's tales, told and remembered and told again. Often they are cautionary tales about all that can go wrong in life. Our grandmothers want the best for us, of course, and the world can be a dangerous place. But the warnings are matched with good, practical advice and the message that it is always possible to set things right, particularly for a girl who carries a ball of yarn and a pair of knitting needles.

How fairy tales are told and remembered has a great deal in common with knitting traditions. It is no mistake that we describe storytelling as knitting a tale, or weaving a story, or spinning a yarn. Writing and knitting share many elements in creating "whole cloth" out of imagination. Both are passed down, within a family or among friends, and often the story or the pattern changes as it moves from person to person. Knitting and writing are both concerned with the process as much as with the end product; the doing and making of something is all-important, and neither is finite. We can always tug and shift yarn to make a garment more our own, a pattern that is uniquely ours, just as we can rewrite a tale so that it is told in our own voice. To be a writer or a knitter, one has to be willing to take things apart and put them back together again. It's hard work to do so, and it takes courage. Patience is required, and the willingness to start over if need be, to rewrite or unravel.

I've always believed that knitting is a good practice for writers and that anyone writing fiction should be taught how to knit. There's much to learn from the perseverance of knitters, their readiness to give themselves over to the process, to enjoy the act of knitting without expectation, to always be willing to change and revise, to make do with what they have, using scraps and bits of pieces that, if they're lucky, may turn out to be glorious. The courage to take apart what you have worked so hard to create is worthy of a fairy tale heroine.

The tradition of the knitting circle as a welcoming place, where a knitter is able to do her work while others are attending to theirs, is legend. How much one can learn from others in such a setting is extraordinary, and merely being in the presence of expert knitters can change the direction of your own creation. This is true for writers' workshops as well. Here, a writer is focused on her own work, but the influences of those around her, particularly those more experienced, affect the writer's work and strengthen it.

Working with my cousin, master knitter Lisa Hoffman, has been a delightful collaboration that began in the pages of *Faerie Magazine*. From the start it was an experiment. Could knitting and storytelling make for a seamless experience? As it turned out, it was not only possible, it was also great fun. We have brought two different types of creativity to a single theme, and in doing so have experienced how one enriches the other. The knitwear brings the story to life, and the story gives meaning to the knitwear. Sometimes the story must change to suit the knitwear; at other times the pattern or yarn is changed to accommodate the story. In the process of working together, our lives and our work became interwoven in a new way. Work enriched our friendship. We learned to speak each other's language.

In each of the stories, knitting figures into the plot and into the lives of the characters. It is what weaves the tales together, and many of the stories feature clever women who use knitting to its best advantage in order to change their fates, win back a lost husband, deal with a wicked queen, or find their way home again.

Fabric arts and storytelling have long been considered women's domains, and so the two seem naturally suited to be together. Both take homespun, homemade things—yarn, the threads of a story—and elevate them into something beautiful and magical. We are indeed spinning straw into gold, beginning with one element and turning it into another. In both knitting and writing, the process is to take the ordinary and make it extraordinary; to make a creation that is both beautiful and useful, a singular object, made by hand, often as a gift for those we love—work that may be done on a snowy evening, by the fireside, where we bring our ideas to life. We create what we imagine. That is the meaning of the oldest magical spell. *Abracadabra.*

That is the magic of storytelling. And the magic of knitting.

Knitting Introduction

Lisa Hoffman

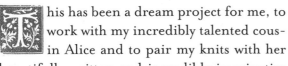

This has been a dream project for me, to work with my incredibly talented cousin Alice and to pair my knits with her beautifully written and incredibly imaginative fairy tales. We began with an idea of collaborating, and every time we came up with a new knit that would work in a story, we were thrilled to discover they fit together perfectly.

The knits in this book are photographed to be illustrative of the stories, to look magical and ethereal, yet each is a wearable or useful item for now and forever. The Invisible Hood is great to pair with a chunky warm sweater on a cool day, or with that one coat you love that just doesn't have its own hood, or the Brokenhearted Vest, which is a great layer over a blouse and jeans. The Thorn Blanket can be knit in many sizes; follow the instructions as written to make a sweet baby blanket, or make it a larger afghan for cuddling under on your couch while binge-watching a favorite TV series. The Amulet Necklace, one of the easiest pieces in the book, is one of my favorites because I've created a template for an art piece that the knitter will personalize as an ornament to wear or to use as art, to hang on a door knob or on a holiday tree.

As a knitwear designer but also as a knitting teacher for many years, I write my patterns as simply and clearly as possible to eliminate any ambiguity in understanding the techniques and methods. By breaking down a pattern to its basic elements, I format each step and give tips on how to best work through the pattern from start to finish. I learn from my students as they learn from me.

I tell my students not to be afraid of what they are doing, but I understand their fear. If they do not completely understand the way the stitches are being formed or if they have not grasped a new technique, they do not feel in control of what is right in their own hands. Like some of the stories in this book, knitting can be a strange and scary endeavor to face, a sort of monster to tackle and to overcome. But it is only yarn and needles, simple and beautiful tools that we can hold and caress and use to create something wonderful.

I love knitting for the sake of the craft. For the interest in design. For the intrigue of how my stitches create art. For the satisfaction of learning and working through a new skill and perfecting it to the best of my ability. I also inherently know that what I do will not be "perfect"; there will be some stitches that are uneven, some rows knit looser or tighter depending on whether I was knitting in the car (in the passenger seat, of course) or in my favorite chair at home. There is sometimes a decrease leaning the wrong way in a lace pattern that I did not notice or an extra row in one glove so it's just a smidge longer than the other. It is a little imbalanced, but I still appreciate what I have achieved. As knitters, we should love the process and not be upset by the little blips along the way. Keep going, use what you have learned, and move on to the next project.

I hope that the pieces in this book bring you joy to work on, pleasure to own, and magic to share.

Chapter 1

Amulet

In the village where they lived, everyone knew there was only one way for a person to be safe from the beast that lived in the woods. Wear an amulet around your neck, and when he comes upon you he will know you are protected. A spell will be broken and you will speak in his language and he will understand yours. But there was more to surviving a meeting such as this. You must be brave. That was the most difficult task.

A map was placed in the center of town charting the way to the home of the beast. All of the men turned away. They had families to look after. None of the boys stepped forward. They had their lessons to think of.

They all stayed behind the walls of their village. This was the season when people shut themselves into their houses, had only soup to eat, and trembled when they heard howling. When the beast came to circle the walls, they tossed out what little they had. Crusts of bread, onion skins, a pot of beans. Still, they shivered and lived in fear. They could not pass the village gates to go into the fields to gather more potatoes and onions. Children had nightmares about teeth and claws. Girls saw no future and refused to fall in love. Young men cursed themselves for having so little courage.

When no one offered to be brave, a lottery was held. They wrote their names on stones and rolled them out on a tabletop to choose their hero. One name came up. Ada. She was the bravest among them, and the strongest.

When she shot an arrow, she always met her mark. When she came upon a mountain, she would swing a rope and climb to the top. Everyone knew she was the only one who could save them.

In truth, her name had been written on every stone.

Her grandmother gave her a meager packet of food, mostly crusts of bread. She dressed Ada in layer after layer of clothing: sweaters, jackets, coats, hats, gloves, mittens. Then she slipped a ribbon around Ada's neck. It was the amulet that would allow her to speak the beast's language and enable him to understand her.

Wearing it, Ada felt no different.

You will feel different, her grandmother told her. *When peril is near, you will hear what you have never heard before, and you will be heard, even by those who have no ears.*

Ada left when the snow was patchy, carrying her bow and arrow. Her grandmother had given her a ball of yarn, saying it was always good luck to travel with one. The farther she went into the woods, the deeper the snow became. It was rough going, even for a girl who climbed mountains. She grew exhausted. She rarely cried, but she was nearly defeated.

How do I go on? she said.

The amulet allowed the oak tree she stood beneath to understand her language. *Take my branches and strap them to your feet.* Ada quickly did so. With her snowshoes she could go more swiftly. To thank the oak, she removed the ax a woodsman had left in its bark, carrying it with her so the tree wouldn't be chopped down.

In the forest, night fell like a curtain. Ada slept beneath some hedges until she heard an owl. She understood its language when it called for her to wake. She could see paw prints as large as a man's hand circled all around her. The prints made a path that had tamped down the snow. To thank the owl, she left the snowshoes she no longer needed so that the branches could be of use for the owl's nest. She went on through what she thought was a field of ice, not realizing that she was crossing a pond. She fell through the ice and might have drowned, had a huge fish not come to her aid. Because Ada could understand its language, she followed beneath the ice, swimming through the cold water until she reached the shallows, where she used the ax to break through the ice. Before she went on she reached into her pockets for the crusts her grandmother had given her so she could thank the fish.

At last she came to the deepest part of the forest. She heard the beast that so terrified the village. But when he howled she understood his language. All at once she knew how lonely it was to be a beast. *Save me from myself,* he said. She followed the path and there he was, a huge wolf.

I've come for you, Ada said.

You? the beast snarled. *Your kind wants to destroy me.*

Ada placed her bow and arrow on the ground.

The beast laughed. *Leave me be,* he said. *Leave me to the misery of being a beast.*

From the east, there came a group of hunters, who began to fire their weapons. The beast was fearsome when he defended himself, even though he was surrounded. Ada grabbed her bow so that she could help chase the men away. When arrows flew, the hunters scattered, back to where they'd come from.

This is what hatred is like, the beast said. *It never stops.*

He led her to the edge of the forest, past the icy pond, where the fish had shown her the way; past the hedges, where the owl had spoken to her; past the oak tree, where the two slept sheltered from a storm. When they reached the outskirts of the town, the beast began to cry. Ada sat down beside him. She thought about her grandmother's advice, how the amulet would make a difference to someone in peril. She slipped it off and strung it around the beast's neck with a bit of her grandmother's yarn, and from then on they understood each other perfectly, for he was a man who'd been under a spell, ruined by hatred, but now was restored by her love.

Amulet Necklace

DIFFICULTY: Beginner

MATERIALS

Tahki Yarns Cotton Classic (108yd/100m, 50g/1.75oz) 100% Mercerized Cotton, 1 skein in color #3724 Leaf Green.
Or approximately 22yd/20m of any DK-weight yarn that meets gauge for each leaf. See Knitting Wisdom for yarn alternatives.

Size 4 (3.5mm) needles or size to obtain gauge.

Assorted feathers, beads, charms, found objects.

Darning needle.

Sewing thread and needle.

Approximately 1.33yd/1.25m of ⅜"/10mm black velvet ribbon or cord for necklace.

SIZES

One size.

FINISHED MEASUREMENTS (FOR SAMPLE SHOWN)

Before finishing: 6½"/16.5cm at widest point, 4"/10cm length.

After finishing: approximately 2½"/6.5cm at widest point, 4"/10cm plus desired length of hanging fringe/beads.

GAUGE

22 sts x 36 rows = 4"/10cm in Seed stitch.
Gauge is not critical, as this is a piece of art, and each amulet will be unique.

Knitting Wisdom

- Use a stiff fiber for a piece that will maintain its shape and have the strength to hold small items sewn or tied to the fabric.

- Alternate fiber options are linen, hemp, flax, even an Icelandic or Shetland wool, or blends of these fibers.

- Be creative by using a hand-dyed or variegated fiber.

- Leave a long yarn tail at cast on and at bind off to use for finishing.

- The amulet is reversible; there is no right side or wrong side to the knitting. After pleating, attach decorations to the preferred side.

STITCH GUIDE

Seed stitch
The Seed stitch pattern is made alternating 1 knit st and 1 purl st across a row and then reversing the sts every row by knitting the purl sts and purling the knit sts.

For more abbreviations, stitches, and techniques, see Glossary.

INSTRUCTIONS

Cast on 37 sts, leaving a long tail to use for finishing.
Set-up row: *K1, p1; rep from * to last st, k1.
Decrease row: K1, k2tog, work in Seed stitch pattern to last 2 sts, k2. 1 st decreased.
Rep decrease row until 4 sts rem.
Next row: K1, k2tog, k1. 3 sts.
Next row: S1, k2tog, psso. 1 st. Cut yarn, leaving a long tail, and pull tail through last st.

FINISHING

If blocking is necessary (depending on choice of fiber), do this before pleating.
Fold cast-on edge accordion style into 3 pleats (see following illustration) and, with yarn from cast on, use a darning needle to sew tightly together through the pleats. This creates a leaf shape. Make a yarn loop at top of pleat and fasten to top of amulet or attach a metal ring. Using yarn tail left hanging from bind off, add additional fringe if desired and/or string with beads or charms of your choice. Attach feathers, charms, buttons, or found objects to amulet with sewing thread. Thread a ribbon through loop or ring at top and tie a knot for desired necklace length.

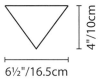

6½"/16.5cm

4"/10cm

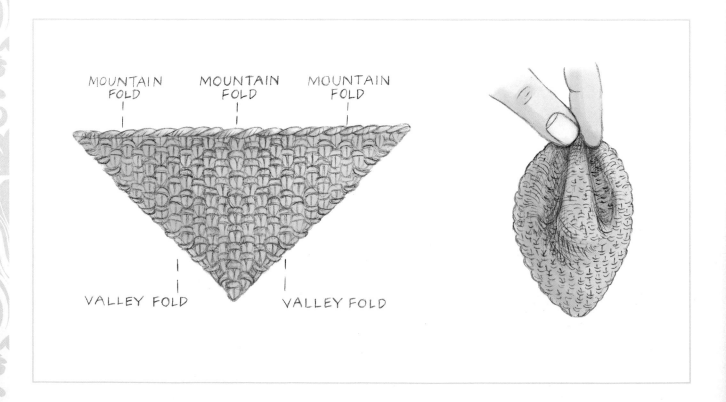

MOUNTAIN FOLD   MOUNTAIN FOLD   MOUNTAIN FOLD

VALLEY FOLD   VALLEY FOLD

Chapter 2
Seventh Sister

he lived in a forest that was so deep no one ever entered or left. A spell had been cast and the trees had grown while she was sleeping. Now she was awake and was a grown woman. When she remembered her dreams, the truth of who she was came back to her. She was the Seventh Sister, led into the woods one dark night. Her sisters had done their best to get rid of her ever since she was a child. First they left her on the edge of a blue lake that was so cold the water could turn blood to ice, but she held on to a log and made her way back and followed them home. The next time they left her on a mountaintop where the billowing clouds were so thick she couldn't see the earth. She followed the path of the wild goats and was home before the others were halfway there.

They were her sisters and she trusted them. How could she know how jealous they were? She had no idea that her father loved her best and planned to give her everything he owned one day. She let them blindfold her and bring her into a cave that was so dark everything inside was the color of the darkest night. When they left her she followed fireflies back up to the surface, and then let the stars show her the way home. The sisters did all they could to lead her astray, but she always found her way back. The kinder she was, the more they despised her. On the day she turned thirteen they cut off all of her hair and dressed her in rags. Still she was beloved. Her father rejoiced and gave her a new dress and a ruby ring, and said she had always brought joy into his life.

That was when her sisters went to the witch. They paid for a potion that would put her to sleep. The price was their beauty. They paid even more dearly for the seeds of the trees that were under a spell and grew without stopping. The price for that was their youth. They took the Seventh Sister into the woods and watched her drink the potion, then they planted the wicked seeds in the ground. Not one of them shed a tear. They were already old and ugly and it was too late for them to undo the price they had paid for their own jealousy.

She might have frozen that first night, and perhaps her sisters wished she had, but the white moths that lived in the woods covered her and kept her warm. For all those enchanted years that she slept, the moths whispered to her in her dreams. *Remember who you are, the Seventh Sister, the one who is loved best of all.*

When she awoke she was a woman, but she thought like a moth. She had bright fluttering ideas of what the future might be. She held no bitterness because her heart was light. She could see through the dark, like a moth. She ate wild apples and drank rainwater. She could hear the trees growing all around her, taller every minute, so dense she couldn't see beyond the ring of grass where she lived. She did not know a town was near, or that there was a blue mountain and a black cave and an icy lake. She didn't know that her sisters had grown even more bitter because their father refused to grant his land to them, insisting he would wait for his youngest daughter's return, leaving a lighted candle in the window each night. She only knew that above her there was a patch of blue. Above there were no branches, only air, and because she thought like a moth, she longed for the sky.

And then one day a terrible chill came, the worst winter storm in a hundred years. The moths covered her to keep her warm, but the cold froze their wings, and that night all the moths dropped to the ground. A wind came from the north, threatening to blow them away. Because she could not bear to lose the creatures that had always protected her, she gathered them together. She took two twigs from the trees that surrounded her and knitted the moths together, even though her fingers bled from the thorns. When she was done, she slipped the cape of wings over her shoulders, weeping for her loss

of the beautiful creatures that had always kept her company. She cried as a moth would, in silence, without tears, but with true sorrow. Then she reached her arms to the sky and rose upward. At last she could see the mountain and the cave and the lake and her father's land.

She went through the dark, the Seventh Sister, the girl who knew what the moths knew, for following the light always led them home. She recognized her house, and when she knocked seven times the door flew open. Her father was so old he thought he was dreaming. He had lit a candle every night in her memory. He thought the moths had flown in, drawn to the light. But it was his daughter, in her cape, and he was right, she had been and was again the joy of his life.

Seventh Sister *Capelet*

DIFFICULTY: Intermediate

MATERIALS

Artyarns Merino Cloud (436yd/400m, 100g/3.5oz) 80% Fine Merino Wool, 20% Cashmere, 1 skein in color #250 Cream. *Or any fingering-weight yarn that meets gauge.*

Size 7 (4.5mm) 24"/60cm circular needles.

Size 8 (5.0mm) 24"/60cm circular needles or size to obtain gauge.

Size 10 (6.0mm) 24"/60cm circular needles.

Cable needle.

Stitch markers.

Darning needle.

SIZES

One size; capelet will stretch generously.

FINISHED MEASUREMENTS

26"/66cm circumference at neck, 48"/122cm circumference at bottom hem, 18"/45.5cm length. Will stretch to fit.

GAUGE

22 sts x 32 rows = 4"/10cm in Moth Lace stitch on size 8 (5.0mm) needles, after blocking.
Take time to check your gauge.

Knitting Wisdom

+ Capelet is worked top down in the round.

+ Row gauges change with the different patterns and needle sizes. Measure as you go and work each pattern as written or to your desired length.

+ Use a different color or shaped stitch marker for beginning of round than those for pattern repeats.

+ This pattern uses a thin yarn with bigger than usual needles. Work loosely so needles can enter stitches without a struggle.

+ Using a lifeline on lace projects is very helpful and can provide a sense of security if placed while working difficult or complex sections where you might need to rip down to fix a mistake. To place a lifeline on a row: Using a thinner yarn in a contrasting color and darning needle, thread a line through all the stitches on the knitting needle at a point where all work is correct. If a mistake is found, work can be dropped down to that point where stitches are saved on the line of contrast yarn. Add more lifelines along the way if desired.

+ Follow the directions for the lace bind-off technique (see Glossary) so that the bottom of the garment has enough stretch.

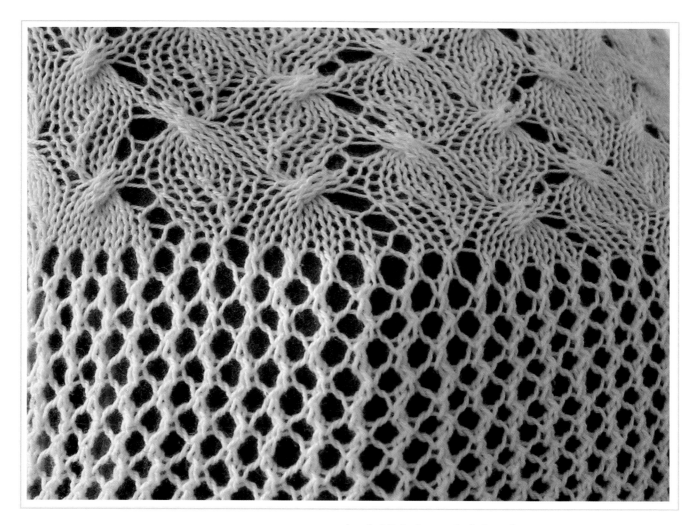

STITCH GUIDE

Broken Rib (worked in the round over a multiple of 4 sts)
Round 1: *K3, p1; rep from * to end.
Round 2: *P1, k1, p2; rep from * to end.

Moth Lace (worked in the round over a multiple of 12 sts)
Round 1: *K2, k2tog, k2, yo, 3/3 LC; rep from * to end.
Round 2 and all even rounds: Knit.
Round 3: *K1, k2tog, k2, yo, k7; rep from * to end.
Round 5: *K2tog, k2, yo, k8; rep from * to end.
Round 7: *3/3 RC, yo, k2, ssk, k2; rep from * to end.
Round 9: *K7, yo, k2, ssk, k1; rep from * to end.
Round 11: *K8, yo, k2, ssk; rep from * to end.
Round 12: Knit.

Openwork Lace (worked in the round over a multiple of 2 sts)
Round 1: *Yo, ssk; rep from * to end.
Round 2: Knit.
Round 3: *K2tog, yo; rep from * to end.
Round 4: Knit.

3/3 LC (3 Over 3 Left Cross)
Slip next 3 sts to cable needle and hold to front, k3, k3 from cable needle.

3/3 RC (3 Over 3 Right Cross)
Slip next 3 sts to cable needle and hold to back, k3, k3 from cable needle.

For more abbreviations, stitches, and techniques, see Glossary.

INSTRUCTIONS

With size 7 (4.5mm) needle, loosely cast on 144 sts. Place marker and join to work in rounds, being careful not to twist sts.

Work rounds 1–2 of Broken Rib 6 times.

Change to size 8 (5.0mm) needle and work rounds 1–12 of Moth Lace 3 times, placing markers every 12 sts for pattern repeats.

Change to size 10 (6.0mm) needle and work rounds 1–12 of Moth Lace 3 more times, removing markers on final round.

Continuing with size 10 (6.0mm) needle, work rounds 1–4 of Openwork Lace 6 times.

Work rounds 1–2 of Broken Rib 4 times.

Bind off using the lace bind-off technique (see Glossary).

FINISHING

Steam or wet block to measurements. Darn ends.

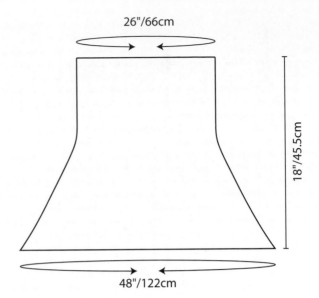

26"/66cm

18"/45.5cm

48"/122cm

Broken Rib Chart

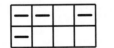

2
1

Openwork Lace Chart

4
3
2
1

Moth Lace Chart

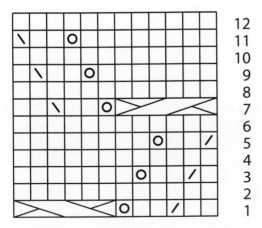

12
11
10
9
8
7
6
5
4
3
2
1

Chart Key

☐ K

⊟ P

☑ K2tog

☒ SSK

◉ YO

⬔ 3/3 RC

⬔ 3/3 LC

Chapter 3

Three Wishes

 year after her mother's passing she still had not gone outside. Now it was winter and the house was encased in ice. She told her husband nothing was wrong, but one day he returned from the marketplace to find her standing outside in her nightgown. She would have frozen had she not been wearing the mittens her mother had knitted for her.

He brought in a wise old woman known for her cures. The two sat beside the fire as the snow fell. The wise woman listened to the wife's heart and heard the break in it. She held her hands and felt they were turning to ice. She noticed that when the wife slipped on her mittens her face was more ruddy, her breathing more even.

There is a way to cure your grief, the wise woman said. *Go out into the snow. You'll find what you need there. Wear your mother's mittens. They will lead you to three pairs of crystals. Each pair will grant a wish. Then your heart's desire will be yours.*

That night in bed, the husband told his wife not to listen to the wise woman. He'd had second thoughts. He insisted it was a mistake to go out in the snow. She would be lost in the woods, where the drifts were deeper than a river. Experienced hunters went out at this time of year and were never seen again; what chance would she have?

All the same, that night, when he was asleep, his wife slipped out of their house. She made her way through snowdrifts, the mittens on her hands keeping her warm. She walked past the road, into the icy fields to where farmers kept their haystacks. Exhausted, she sat down. She felt hopeless and wondered if, indeed, she had made a mistake. But then she felt something in the haystack. Two crystals. They shimmered in the palm of her hand. She wished she could see her mother one last time, even though she knew it was impossible. She fell asleep in the haystack, and as she slept her wish came true, for her mother came to her in her dreams. *Sew the crystals to your mittens and you will receive your heart's desire. But remember, I am the past. You must wish for the future.*

She found her way home and sat at the table with a needle and thread, sewing the crystals to the mittens. When her husband awoke he would not have known she had gone out except that the hem of her nightgown had turned to ice.

The next night he locked the door. There had been more snow, and drifts covered the windows. *You cannot find a cure in a storm,* the man told his wife.

All the same, when he fell asleep, she used her mother's knitting needle to pry open the lock. The snow made it difficult to walk in the woods, but soon she found a path the deer had made. She followed it until she came to a tall pine tree. There among the roots of the tree were two more crystals that shone like stars. She wished that her husband could understand her. When she fell asleep beneath the tree, she dreamed that he knew her better than she knew herself. *I am your present,* he said in her dream. *I know your heart's desire is in the future.*

She returned home as the sun was rising, her boots coated with ice. Her husband was at the door waiting for her. He'd been there all night, worrying. *I cannot lose you,* he pleaded.

You won't, she told him. *But you must let me go one more time.*

The following night her husband gave her a lantern, a new coat to keep her warm, and his own boots. When he kissed her she knew that he understood her.

I'll be back, she promised.

She went even farther this night. The moon was full and the world shimmered with light. She walked past fields, and frozen streams, and towns where everyone was asleep in their beds. In a tiny village she came to a pond where children often skated. It was deserted now, but she sat on a bench where many children had stopped to tie their skates. When she reached down she found two more crystals, brighter than the moon. That night when she fell asleep on the bench, she dreamed a little girl had come to stand beside her. They watched the ice on the pond as it melted. They watched the grass turn green. The little girl took her hand and together they took a step into the future, where there was as much happiness as there was grief.

In the morning it took a long time for her to find her way, so long that the snow melt-ed and the world became bright. At last she reached home. She sat on the porch and sewed on the last two crystals. Her husband came outside to sit beside her and hold her hand. By next winter they would have a little girl, her heart's desire, a child whose hair was as pale as snow. As soon as the child was old enough she would wear the mittens her grandmother had knitted, and no matter what winter might bring, she would never be cold.

❧

Three Wishes Mittens

DIFFICULTY: Intermediate

MATERIALS

Brooklyn Tweed Shelter (140yd/128m, 50g/1.75oz) 100% American Targhee-Columbia Wool, 2 skeins in color Sweatshirt. *Or any worsted-weight yarn that meets gauge.*

Size 7 (4.5mm) double-point needles or size to obtain gauge.

Size 4 (3.5mm) double-point needles.

Cable needle.

Stitch holder or scrap yarn for thumb gusset stitches.

Darning needle.

Stitch markers.

Six buttons, approximately ¾"/2mm each.

SIZES

One size.

FINISHED MEASUREMENTS

12½"/32cm length, 8"/20.5cm circumference at palm.

GAUGE

16 sts x 24 rows = 4"/10cm in Stockinette stitch on larger needles, after blocking.
Take time to check your gauge.

Knitting Wisdom

- ✦ Pattern is written for working on double-point needles but can easily be adapted for 2 circulars or Magic Loop methods.

- ✦ When joining after cast on, attach a split ring or locking stitch marker directly to your work for beginning of round.

- ✦ For left mitten, beginning of round marker shifts before and after removing thumb gusset stitches.

- ✦ Use different colored or shaped markers for beginning of round, gusset, and cable panel.

- ✦ Changing needle size is an easy way to shape at the wrists for a comfortable fit without having to increase and decrease stitches.

STITCH GUIDE

Garter stitch (worked in the round)
Round 1: Purl.
Round 2: Knit.

Stockinette stitch (worked in the round)
Knit every round.

Crystal Cables (over 7 sts)
Round 1: K1, 1/1 RPC, p1, 1/1 LPC, k1.
Round 2: K2, p3, k2.
Round 3: 1/1 RPC, p3, 1/1 LPC.
Round 4: K1, p5, k1.
Round 5: K1, p5, k1.
Round 6: K1, p5, k1.
Round 7: 1/1 LC, p3, 1/1 RC.
Round 8: K2, p3, k2.
Round 9: K1, 1/1 LC, p1, 1/1 RC, k1.
Round 10: K3, p1, k3.
Round 11: K3, p1, k3.

1/1 LC (1 Over 1 Left Cross)
Slip next st to cable needle and hold to front, k1, k1 from cable needle.

1/1 LPC (1 Over 1 Left Purl Cross)
Slip next st to cable needle and hold to front, p1, k1 from cable needle.

1/1 RC (1 Over 1 Right Cross)
Slip next st to cable needle and hold to back, k1, k1 from cable needle.

1/1 RPC (1 Over 1 Right Purl Cross)
Slip next st to cable needle and hold to back, k1, p1 from cable needle.

For more abbreviations, stitches, and techniques, see Glossary.

INSTRUCTIONS FOR RIGHT MITTEN

Cuff
With larger needles, cast on 34 sts and divide onto 3 needles (15 sts/9 sts/10 sts). Place BOR marker and join to work in rounds. Work in Garter stitch for 16 rounds (approximately 1¾"/4.5cm).
Change to Stockinette stitch for 16 rounds.
Change to smaller needles. Knit 8 rounds.

Change back to larger needles. Knit 8 rounds.

Thumb gusset with pattern
Set-up round 1: K5, place panel marker, k7, place panel marker, k4, place gusset marker, M1R, k2, M1L, place gusset marker, knit to end.
Set-up round 2: Knit 1 round, slipping all markers.
Round 1: K5, sm, work round 1 of Crystal Cables, sm, k4, sm, M1R, knit to marker, M1L, sm, knit to end.
Round 2: K5, sm, work round 2 of Crystal Cables, sm, knit to end.
Round 3: K5, sm, work Crystal Cables, sm, k4, sm, M1R, knit to marker, M1L, sm, knit to end.
Round 4: K5, sm, work Crystal Cables, sm, knit to end.
Rep rounds 3 and 4 two more times.
Next round: K5, sm, work Crystal Cables, sm, k4, place 12 gusset sts on holder or scrap yarn for thumb, remove gusset markers, use thumb cast-on method to cast on 2 sts, knit to end. 34 sts.
Next round: Knit to panel marker, sm, work Crystal Cables, sm, knit to end.

Hand
Work even as established until rounds 1–11 of Crystal Cables have been worked a total of 3 times. At this point, glove should meet top of index finger. To make longer, rep last round to desired length.

Decrease
Remove panel markers on next round, redistributing sts as needed to work decreases.
Decrease round 1: K1, ssk, k5, p1, k5, k2tog, k1, place marker, k1, ssk, k11, k2tog, k1. 30 sts.
Decrease round 2: K1, ssk, k4, p1, k4, k2tog, k1, sm, k1, ssk, k9, k2tog, k1. 26 sts.
Decrease round 3: K1, ssk, k3, p1, k3, k2tog, k1, sm, k1, ssk, k7, k2tog, k1. 22 sts.
Decrease round 4: K1, ssk, k2, p1, k2, k2tog, k1, sm, k1, ssk, k5, k2tog, k1. 18 sts.

Decrease round 5: K1, ssk, k1, p1, k1, k2tog, k1, sm, k1, ssk, k3, k2tog, k1. 14 sts.
Decrease round 6: K1, ssk, p1, k2tog, k1, sm, k1, ssk, k1, k2tog, k1. 10 sts.
Place 5 sts each onto 2 dpns, close top with Kitchener stitch.

Thumb
Divide 12 held thumb sts evenly onto 3 needles. Rejoin yarn at gusset and knit 1 round, picking up 2 sts in 2 cast-on sts at top of thumb space; place marker for new BOR. 14 sts. Join and knit for 12 rounds (approximately 1½"/4cm) or until thumb is ½"/1.5cm shorter than desired length.
Decrease round 1: K2tog, *k1, k2tog; rep from * to end. 9 sts.
Decrease round 2: K1, *k2tog; rep from * to end. 5 sts.
Cut yarn. With darning needle, thread tail through rem sts and gather to close top of thumb.

INSTRUCTIONS FOR LEFT MITTEN

Cuff
With larger needles, cast on 34 sts and divide onto 3 needles (14 sts/10 sts/10 sts). Place BOR marker and join to work in rounds. Work in Garter stitch for 16 rounds (approximately 1¾"/4.5cm).
Change to Stockinette stitch for 16 rounds.
Change to smaller needles. Knit 8 rounds.
Change back to larger needles. Knit 8 rounds, end last round 4 sts before marker.

Thumb gusset with pattern
Set-up round 1: Place new BOR marker, k3, place gusset marker, M1R, k2 (removing old BOR marker), M1L, place gusset marker, k4, place cable panel marker, k7, place cable panel marker, knit to end.
Set-up round 2: Knit 1 round, slipping all markers.

Round 1: K3, sm, M1R, knit to marker, M1L, sm, k4, sm, work round 1 of Crystal Cables, sm, knit to end.

Round 2: Knit to panel marker, sm, work round 2 of Crystal Cables, sm, knit to end.

Round 3: K3, sm, M1R, knit to marker, M1L, sm, k4, sm, work Crystal Cables, sm, knit to end.

Round 4: Knit to panel marker, sm, work Crystal Cables, sm, knit to end. Rep rounds 3 and 4 two more times.

Next round: Remove BOR marker, k3, place 12 gusset sts on holder or scrap yarn for thumb, remove gusset markers, use thumb cast-on method to cast on 1 st, place new BOR marker, cast on 1 st, knit to panel marker, work Crystal Cables, sm, knit to end. 34 sts.

Next round: Knit to marker, sm, work Crystal Cables, sm, knit to end.

Hand
Complete as for right mitten.

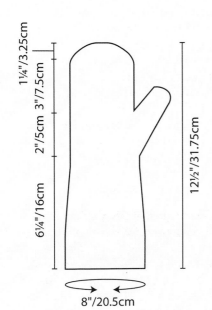

FINISHING

Darn all ends. Sew buttons to circular spaces in Crystal Cables panel on back of each hand.

Crystal Cables Chart

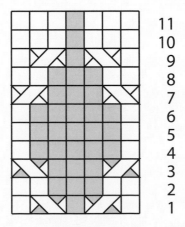

Crystal Cables Chart Key

□	K
▦	P
⧄	1/1 RC
⧅	1/1 LC
⧄	1/1 RPC
⧅	1/1 LPC

Chapter 4

The Lilac Tree

he had lost everything, but what is lost can also be found.

Her husband had gone off to war. He promised he would return, but years had passed. Time was like a river that washed over her, and now there was gray in her hair.

On summer days she stood beneath the lilac tree where she had met him when they weren't much more than children. Now that time was long ago. Nothing bloomed anymore. There had been a great drought, and the land had parched as the war dragged on. Everyone in the village had left and moved away. Except for her.

She was waiting for him.

Every day she was there beneath the tree as the leaves fell off one by one and the seasons changed. She sat in the grass and knitted a scarf, but as time moved forward the scarf became a shawl. By the time she was done there was snow on the ground.

He had been gone for years. Perhaps he'd been captured, or lost in the desert. The king himself had fled to another country, one where there was rain and everything bloomed with a haze of violet and green. The war was over and there was nothing to fight for anymore. People's lives had been ruined and saved; villages had been burned and rebuilt.

But her husband had still not returned.

She stood beneath the lilac tree even in winter, when the bark was black and the boughs were thick with snow. She thought about the first time she saw him, the first time she talked to him, the first time he kissed her, when the lilacs were fragrant and new. In the evenings the edges of the blooms turned violet. She wrapped herself in the shawl and closed her eyes. When she opened them again the snow had disappeared, the lilacs were blooming, and her husband was walking down the lane toward her.

How had this happened? Had time shifted into the future? She didn't care. All she knew was that her husband was close by.

She raced toward him, but as she ran her shawl fell from her shoulders. The world turned cold in that instant. She was back on that wintery day when no lilacs bloomed, shivering and alone. The shawl fell into a snowdrift. Before she could grab it, it had disappeared. No matter how deeply she dug, she couldn't find it.

Somehow she had knitted the future into the shawl, and without it, time would not move forward. Every day was the same, filled with darkness and snow. Every day she tried to recover the scarf, but she had no luck at all. Winter lasted for four months, and then five months, and then a year.

Every night she was alone in the home they had once shared. She had her dinner, always saving her crumbs for the mouse that lived under the stone hearth. Because the woman had been so kind, the mouse decided to return the favor. He crept into her coat pocket, and when she went out the next day he went along, riding in her pocket, where he was glad to find crumbs.

The woman knelt in the snow beneath the lilac tree, searching for the shawl as she did every day. By now the drifts were as tall as a man and the cold, blue snow seemed as if it would never melt.

The mouse jumped into the snow. The drift was so dark and so deep it was as if night had fallen, the blue night of winter. Still, he followed his nose. He picked up the scent of lilacs, and before long he found the scarf. It was too heavy for him to carry so he did the best he could. He took a single thread.

When he presented the thread, the woman cried and her tears melted the snow. There was the shawl that held her future. She placed it around her shoulders. Now when she looked across the field the grass was green. The future had arrived. There was her husband, after all this time, coming back to her on the day when the lilacs finally bloomed.

❧

Lilac Tree *Scarf*

DIFFICULTY: Advanced beginner

MATERIALS

The Periwinkle Sheep Sport Wolle (325yd/297m, 3.5oz/100g) 100% Wool, 4 skeins: 1 in color Ghost of Molly [A], 2 in color Hyacinth [B], 1 in color Slate [C].
Or approximately 1,300yd/1,188m total of any sport-weight yarn that meets gauge.

Size 5 (3.75mm) needles or size to obtain gauge.

J-10/6mm crochet hook or larger for attaching fringe.

Darning needle.

SIZES

One size.

FINISHED MEASUREMENTS

14"/35.5cm width, 69"/175.5cm length.

GAUGE

23 sts x 34 rows = 4"/10cm in Basket stitch, after blocking.
23 sts x 34 rows = 4"/10cm in Stockinette stitch/Reverse Stockinette stitch, after blocking.
Take time to check your gauge.

Knitting Wisdom

- ✦ Scarf has Reverse Stockinette edges on the sides that will curl toward the right side of work, and on the top and bottom that will curl toward the wrong side of work.

- ✦ When transitioning between colors DO NOT CUT YARN until after working second repeat of pattern row 8. Carry alternate color up along the edge with an even tension so fabric doesn't pull.

- ✦ To cut strands for fringe tassels, use a book that is approximately the length or width of the finished measurement and wrap yarn around loosely for the desired number of strands, then cut through them all at once—you will have a doubled length that will be halved when folded and pulled through to knot.

- ✦ Leave enough of desired color to cut strands for fringe tassels (I used about ¼ of a skein, approximately 85yd/77.5m for tassels on the sample shown) or cut them in advance to be sure to have enough.

- ✦ Use this or a similar, handwritten chart to note your color choices:

A	
B	
C	

STITCH GUIDE

Reverse Stockinette stitch
Row 1 (RS): Purl.
Row 2 (WS): Knit.

Basket stitch (multiple of 10 + 15) (includes edge sts)
Row 1 (RS): P6, *k3, p7; rep from * to last 9 sts, k3, p6.
Row 2 (WS): K6, p3, *k7, p3; rep from * to last 6 sts, k6.
Row 3: Rep row 1.
Row 4: K6, purl to last 6 sts, k6.
Row 5: P11, *k3, p7; rep from * to last 14 sts, k3, p11.
Row 6: K11, p3, *k7, p3; rep from * to last 11 sts, k11.
Row 7: Rep row 5.
Row 8: Rep row 4.

For more abbreviations, stitches, and techniques, see Glossary.

INSTRUCTIONS

With A, cast on 85 sts. Beginning with a RS purl row, work 6 rows in Reverse Stockinette stitch.
Work rows 1–8 of Basket stitch 19 times or until piece measures approximately 18"/45.5cm, ending with row 8 of Basket stitch.

Transition to next color by alternating colors as follows (see Knitting Wisdom):
With B, work rows 1 and 2 of Basket stitch.
With A, work rows 3 and 4 of Basket stitch.
With B, work rows 5 and 6 of Basket stitch.
With A, work rows 7 and 8 of Basket stitch.
Rep previous 8 rows once more.

Cut A, continue with B. Work Basket stitch (rows 1–8) 30 more times or until piece measures approximately 48"/122cm, ending with row 8 of Basket stitch.

Transition to next color by alternating colors as follows (see Knitting Wisdom):
With C, work rows 1 and 2 of Basket stitch.
With B, work rows 3 and 4 of Basket stitch.
With C, work rows 5 and 6 of Basket stitch.
With B, work rows 7 and 8 of Basket stitch.
Rep previous 8 rows once more.

Cut B, continue with C. Work rows 1–8 of Basket stitch 18 more times or until piece measures approximately 67"/170cm, ending with row 8 of Basket stitch. Work rows 1–7 of Basket stitch once more.
Beginning with a WS knit row, work 6 rows in Reverse Stockinette stitch. Bind off.

FINISHING

Darn ends. Steam lightly. Make four large fringe tassels (see Fringe Tassels note) and attach one at each corner.

FRINGE TASSELS

For each tassel, cut forty 14"/35.5cm strands. With RS of work facing, insert crochet hook in corner of scarf from back to front, grab middle of all strands together and pull loop through to back, then pull that loop over the remaining ends toward the front. Tighten and adjust to neaten. Rep in each of the remaining corners.

Basket Stitch Chart

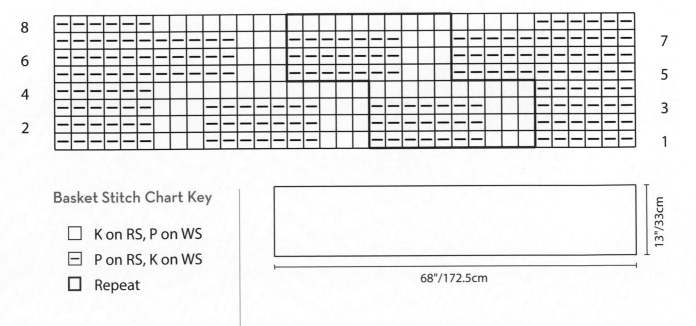

Basket Stitch Chart Key

☐ K on RS, P on WS

⊟ P on RS, K on WS

☐ Repeat

13"/33cm

68"/172.5cm

Chapter 5

Love Never Ending

t first she didn't know a spell had been cast upon her husband. They had known one another since they were children. They'd grown up together and went to school together and loved only each other and had married young. Their lives had been braided together through good times and bad. For years they had been not only lovers but also best friends. There had never been an unkind word or argument between them. Then the woman began to notice small changes. They were so tiny, like moths in the palm of her hand, but fluttering, all the same, full of life.

The first change was that he could not sleep. He, who had always slept like a rock, now left their bed when the stars came out to wander through the woods. He lost interest in their farm. The fields were left untended, and the cows came to the barn crying to be milked. He stared at the pastures as if they belonged to someone else, and were nothing more than a bother.

Now he did not answer when she spoke to him. He did not even seem to hear her. His thoughts were elsewhere; he seemed to speak another language, one she had never learned. He said words she hadn't heard him say before: *betrayal, secret, lie.*

I need to think, he told her. *I need to be alone.*

He refused the meals she offered him, even when she cooked his favorite dishes. Usually he traipsed through the mud on his daily rounds of the farm. Now he came home from his walks with his boots neatly polished to a fine shine, as if by magic. He wore a sweater she had never seen before. One day his pale blue eyes turned green.

Then she knew. Something had begun.

She went across the meadow to her dearest friend's house, a friend so dear she was called Darling, for she was that sweet and good. She could always be called upon to visit on dark days, to join them for dinner, to bring flowers and herbs as gifts. The woman told Darling of her fears. When something was begun, something else was ending. She was losing her husband a little more each day.

It's the witch, Darling told her. Darling was plain looking, but she dressed well. She wore silk dresses, and she always made certain her black leather boots were polished to a fine shine. *The witch has enchanted him. You must go to her and beg her to let him be.* The dear friend gave her a small bottle. *Drink this when you're in the witch's presence and it will protect you from harm and force her to tell you the truth.*

The very next day the woman went to the twisted tree where the witch had lived for a hundred years. Everyone knew the witch was best left alone. Witches are easily angered, and one never knows how they will react to an accusation; still, the woman who was losing her husband was desperate. She knocked on the oak door. No one answered, so she let herself inside. There was the witch at her spinning wheel. The yarn she spun first appeared to be the color of the earth, then it shifted to the color of the meadows in spring, then at last it became the color of the tree where the witch lived.

Who asked you to come here? the witch said.

Please, the woman begged, *let me have my husband back. Don't take him from me.*

You can have him, the witch told her. *I never wanted a husband. How dare you accuse me!*

The woman reached into her pocket and took out the bottle that Darling had given her for protection. When she opened it the room smelled like almonds. Just as she was about to drink, the witch threw a knitting needle that shattered the bottle. As it spilled, the liquid burned everything it touched. Sparks of the poisonous fire of envy fell around her onto the earthen floor.

Whoever gave that potion is the one who is enchanting your husband, the witch said. *She wished to do away with you so she could have him for her own and I would be the one who was blamed for your death.*

The witch and the young woman sat at the table. They had become allies. The witch mixed up a tea ground from the leaves of the tree that was her home. The fragrant green tea would make the husband sleep for as long as Darling's spell was upon him. *While he sleeps this is what you must do if you still want this man. Why you would, I'm not certain. But love is a curious thing.*

I want him, the young woman said, for she'd known him for what seemed like forever, long before he'd been enchanted.

Knit a circle and do not stop. Knit it as long as infinity, for love that is true never dies, and love that is meant to be cannot be stolen.

The young woman took the yarn the witch gave her. It was made with the sort of love that could defeat envy. She gave her husband the tea and he fell into a deep, untroubled sleep. Then she set about knitting. On some nights she heard footsteps outside. They circled the cottage. She knew who was there and she knew what she wanted, but the young woman just continued to knit. On other nights someone beat her fists against the door. She heard her dearest friend's voice calling to her husband, but she didn't answer. She kept knitting without bothering to rest. She knitted through the summer and into the fall, and then it was winter and she was finally done. She looped the cowl around her throat and woke her husband. When he saw her he recognized the way she loved him and he remembered that he loved her in return. They never spoke about the friend again, and they never saw her either, nor did anyone else in their town, although the old witch sometimes came to the market wearing good black leather boots, polished to a fine shine.

ৈ.

Love Never Ending *Cowl*

DIFFICULTY: Intermediate

MATERIALS

Lorna's Laces Shepherd Worsted (225yd/205.5m, 4oz/113g) 100% Superwash Merino Wool, 3 skeins in color #609 Fiddlehead.
Or any worsted-weight yarn that meets gauge.

Size 8 (5.0mm) 16"/40cm circular needles or size to obtain gauge.

Stitch marker.

Darning needle.

SIZES

One size.

FINISHED MEASUREMENTS

6"/15cm width, 68"/172.5cm length before seaming.

GAUGE

20 sts x 26 rounds = 4"/10cm in Stockinette stitch, after blocking. *Take time to check your gauge.*

Knitting Wisdom

- ✦ The cowl is knit in rounds, creating a hollow tube with the Leafstalk Lace panel twisting around it. The cast-on and bound-off edges are joined to create a circular cowl.

- ✦ If desired, a provisional cast on may be used, and the cowl can be joined using the Kitchener stitch.

- ✦ Each odd-numbered round increases 1 stitch within the lace pattern. The following even-numbered round ends with a decrease. After working 2 rounds, the stitch count is unchanged. Because the cowl starts with a set-up round, which includes a decrease, the final even round omits its decrease.

INSTRUCTIONS

Cast on 68 sts. Place marker and join to work in rounds, being careful not to twist sts. Knit to last 2 sts, k2tog.
Round 1: Work round 1 of Leafstalk Lace, knit to end.
Round 2 and all even rounds: Work round 2 of Leafstalk Lace, knit to last 2 sts, k2tog.
Round 3: Work round 3 of Leafstalk Lace, knit to end. Continue as established until rounds 1–10 of Leafstalk Lace have been worked 39 times or to desired length, eliminating k2tog from final repeat of round 10. Bind off.

FINISHING

Turn work inside out to darn ends on WS where skeins were joined. Turn back to RS. Steam or block to desired measurements. Sew cast-on edge to bound-off edge, matching sts at Leafstalk Lace panel.

STITCH GUIDE

Leafstalk Lace (over 20 sts)
Round 1: P3, k6, k3tog, yo, k1, yo, p3, ssk, yo, k1, yo.
Round 2 and all even rounds (WS): P3, k10, p3, k4.
Round 3: P3, k4, k3tog, k1, yo, k1, yo, k1, p3, ssk, yo, k1, yo.
Round 5: P3, k2, k3tog, k2, yo, k1, yo, k2, p3, ssk, yo, k1, yo.
Round 7: P3, k3tog, k3, yo, k1, yo, k3, p3, ssk, yo, k1, yo.
Round 9: P3, k10, p3, ssk, yo, k1, yo.
Round 10: P3, k10, p3, k4.

For more abbreviations, stitches, and techniques, see Glossary.

Leafstalk Lace Chart

Leafstalk Lace Chart (rows 1–10, read right to left). Symbols per the key below; blank squares = K.

Row	1	2	3	4	5	6	7	8	9	10	11	12	13	14	15	16	17	18	19
10																	−	−	−
9	O		O	\	−	−	−										−	−	−
8					−	−	−										−	−	−
7	O		O	\	−	−	−				O		O			/3	−	−	−
6					−	−	−										−	−	−
5	O		O	\	−	−	−			O		O			/3		−	−	−
4					−	−	−										−	−	−
3	O		O	\	−	−	−		O		O		/3				−	−	−
2					−	−	−										−	−	−
1	O		O	\	−	−	−	O		O	/3						−	−	−

Leafstalk Lace Chart Key

- □ K
- − P
- \ SSK
- /3 K3tog
- ⊙ YO

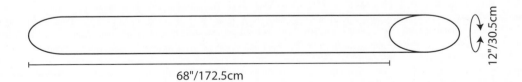

68"/172.5cm

12"/30.5cm

Chapter 6

Blue Heron

She was the youngest daughter and no one noticed her. She was not beautiful, but she was quiet and kind. She excelled at quiet things: cooking, fishing, walking through the marsh at dusk. She spent her evenings knitting, using two twigs she'd found in the woods as her needles, spinning the wool she was given from a neighbor's sheep in exchange for chores. She helped her six sisters in all things and did as her father told her. But there was one thing about her no one who knew her would have guessed.

She had a secret.

From the time her mother died, when she was eight years old, she had journeyed into the marsh in the evenings.

She had run off crying after her mother's funeral. No one had noticed her missing. They were visiting with the neighbors, eating a cold supper, but she was devastated. Without her mother, there was no one who loved her or knew her for the person she was. She ran until she was lost. To see where she was, she climbed high into a tree. But the night was too dark to spy the path she had taken, and she soon fell asleep. When she awoke she discovered that she was in the nest of a heron, surrounded by its fledglings. When the mother heron arrived home she felt compassion for the strange girl fledgling she discovered, perhaps because she was featherless and defenseless. She let the girl who was so full of sorrow sleep under her wing. Every night the girl came to the heron's nest, and even when the

chicks grew up and flew away, she slept there. She stayed until the weather turned chilly and the time came when all herons must leave for warmer climates.

The girl knitted a shawl of feathers from the ones her heron sisters and brothers had left behind. She wanted to make certain that her heron mother would not worry because her skin was bare. By now there was ice on the water, and her heron mother had no choice but to fly away. They both cried when they parted, for herons have hearts that allow them to love what is quiet and kind.

Every spring the girl waited for her heron mother's return, wearing the shawl of feathers. She helped to raise the new fledglings. Each time a new group left, she stood on the edge of the huge nest woven of twigs and moss and wished she could fly away with them. In her human life, each of her six sisters was married by now, and her father was old, a hundred at least. Years passed and she was now a woman, one who carried the secret of the other life she led close to her heart.

One morning when she came home her father confronted her: Where had she been? Why were there feathers in her hair? Mud on her feet? A string of fish she'd caught, ready for cooking? Why was she always disappearing?

She could not explain, so he decided she was up to no good and it was time for her to be wed. He arranged a marriage for her with a man who ran the lumber mill that cut down trees in the marsh. She hated him before she met him, for she had the emotions of a heron, and herons love trees as much as they love flying through the air. The Mill Owner came to supper; he looked her up and down, felt her leg, then said he'd have her. She cried all that night in the nest in the marsh. Throughout the years her heron mother had learned bits of her language. She knew certain human words: *love, sorrow, kindness, comfort, fish, feather, fan.*

Before you marry, she told her human daughter, *slip on the shawl.*

The wedding was held in a hall in town made of stone and bricks. Her six sisters, who had always ignored her, were there with their husbands and children. The Mill Owner looked older and meaner in the bright daylight. The girl who had lived with herons wore a plain blue dress. She asked that all the windows be left open, for it was a warm day. She wanted sunlight, blue sky, escape. There was a wedding cake on the table. The girl had made it herself, knowing she would never taste a bite. Let the neighbors devour it; let them eat every crumb. When she and the Mill Owner stood before the reverend, the girl wrapped the shawl of feathers around her shoulders. She felt a freedom inside her, the taste of the salt in the marsh. Afterward, people said she rose up and left through the window; some even said

she had become a bird, a beautiful blue bird as large as a woman. Her nieces and nephews swore they found feathers on the floor.

She went back to the marsh. She knew the way by heart. She found an inlet where no one without tall boots and a map would ever find her. A fisherman saw her take off her shawl and thought she was beautiful and kind and quiet. She lives with him in a cottage right next to the water, so they can catch fish from their front porch. There she found sunlight and blue sky and freedom. In the dusk of evening, she kisses her fisherman before she throws her shawl over her shoulders and goes to visit her heron mother. Her husband trusts her to come back by morning, and she always does. Some people say that if you walk through the marsh at midnight you may spy two blue herons, a mother and a daughter, mending their nest of twigs, and if you're fortunate enough to find one of their feathers, you can weave it into your own shawl. Then, every night, you will dream the same dream the herons do.

Blue Heron *Shawl*

DIFFICULTY: Advanced

MATERIALS

Prism Radiant Petite Madison Layers (372yd/340m, 100g/3.5oz) 73% Merino, 7% Cashmere, 10% Silk, 10% Stellina SPK, 3 skeins in color Platinum. *Or any sport-weight yarn that meets gauge.*

Size 5 (3.75mm) 24"/60cm and 32"/80cm circular needles or size to obtain gauge.

Darning needle.

SIZES

One size; change size by varying gauge and/or number of pattern repeats.

FINISHED MEASUREMENTS

80"/203cm width, 38"/96.5cm length of center spine from cast on to center point bind off, after blocking.

GAUGE

26 sts x 30 rows = 4"/10cm in Feather Lace stitch, after blocking. 27 sts x 30 rows = 4"/10cm in Stockinette stitch, after blocking. *Take time to check your gauge.*

Knitting Wisdom

+ On right side, slip first stitch knitwise with yarn in back; on wrong side, slip first stitch purlwise with yarn in front.

+ After row 3, pattern increases 4 stitches every right side row.

+ After row 11, pattern reveals itself and new tiers (feathers) are created every 8 rows.

+ Change to 32"/80cm needle when needed.

+ It is impossible to use fixed stitch markers on this project, as the stitches are constantly shifting with increases and decreases every other row. Let the yarn overs be the guide for counting tiers. If needed, place a removable or locking stitch marker on the center stitch and move it up every few rows.

+ This pattern doesn't lend itself to a chart because of the shifting stitches. Refer to the written directions.

+ The sample Blue Heron Shawl is 30 tiers in Feather Lace; the center point adds an additional 9 rows.

+ Whatever yarn weight you choose, work a gauge swatch before beginning the full project, because when working on a circular needle, unless you transfer stitches to a strand of yarn, you will not be able to lay the shawl flat to measure your work.

+ Work a swatch of 5 tiers (45 rows/95 stitches) and work the Feather Tip bind off. Measure the center spine for row gauge and along cast-on edge for stitch gauge. Each tier adds 8 rows and 16 stitches, so do the math from your swatch gauge to determine the desired size for your finished shawl.

+ Your stitch count, after completing a pattern row 8, will be as follows: 3 (edge stitches) + multiples of 8 (# of tiers along one side) + 9 (center stitches) + multiples of 8 (# of tiers along other side) + 3 (edge stitches) = your current stitch count. With 30 tiers complete, the sample ends with 3 + 240 + 9 + 240 + 3 = 495 stitches before binding off.

STITCH GUIDE

Feather Lace

Each 8-row repeat creates one tier. Sts in brackets will repeat as stitch count increases in pattern.

Row 1 (RS): S1 knitwise, k1, yo, p1, [k6, k2tog, yo], k4, yo, k1, yo, k4, [yo, ssk, k6], p1, yo, k2.

Row 2 and all WS rows: S1 purlwise, purl to end.

Row 3: S1, k1, yo, p1, [k6, k2tog, yo], k6, yo, k1, yo, k6, [yo, ssk, k6], p1, yo, k2.

Row 5: S1, k1, yo, p1, [k6, k2tog, yo], k7, yo, k3, yo, k7, [yo, ssk, k6], p1, yo, k2.

Row 7: S1, k1, yo, p1, [k6, k2tog, yo], k2, KYOK (see Glossary), k2, [yo, ssk, k6], p1, yo, k2.

Row 8: S1, purl to end.

For more abbreviations, stitches, and techniques, see Glossary.

INSTRUCTIONS

Cast on 5 sts.

Row 1 (RS): S1 knitwise, k1, yo, k1, yo, k2. 7 sts.

Row 2 and all WS rows: S1 purlwise, purl to end.

Row 3: S1, [k1, yo] 4 times, k2. 11 sts.

Row 5: S1, k1, yo, p1, k2, KYOK, k2, p1, yo, k2. 15 sts.

Row 7: S1, k1, yo, p1, k4, yo, k1, yo, k4, p1, yo, k2. 19 sts.

Row 9: S1, k1, yo, p1, k6, yo, k1, yo, k6, p1, yo, k2. 23 sts.

Row 11: S1, k1, yo, p1, k7, yo, k3, yo, k7, p1, yo, k2. 27 sts.

Row 13: S1, k1, yo, p1, k6, k2tog, yo, k2, KYOK, k2, yo, ssk, k6, p1, yo, k2. 31 sts.

Row 15: S1, k1, yo, p1, k6, k2tog, yo, k4, yo, k1, yo, k4, yo, ssk, k6, p1, yo, k2. 35 sts.

Row 17: S1, k1, yo, p1, k6, k2tog, yo, k6, yo, k1, yo, k6, yo, ssk, k6, p1, yo, k2. 39 sts.

Row 19: S1, k1, yo, p1, k6, k2tog, yo, k7, yo, k3, yo, k7, yo, ssk, k6, p1, yo, k2. 43 sts.

Row 21: S1, k1, yo, p1, [k6, k2tog, yo] 2 times, k2, KYOK, k2, [yo, ssk, k6] 2 times, p1, yo, k2. 47 sts.

Row 23: S1, k1, yo, p1, [k6, k2tog, yo] 2 times, k4, yo, k1, yo, k4, [yo, ssk, k6] 2 times, p1, yo, k2. 51 sts.

Row 25: S1, k1, yo, p1, [k6, k2tog, yo] 2 times, k6, yo, k1, yo, k6, [yo, ssk, k6] 2 times, p1, yo, k2. 55 sts.

Row 27: S1, k1, yo, p1, [k6, k2tog, yo] 2 times, k7, yo, k3, yo, k7, [yo, ssk, k6] 2 times, p1, yo, k2. 59 sts.

Row 29: S1, k1, yo, p1, [k6, k2tog, yo] 3 times, k2, KYOK, k2, [yo, ssk, k6] 3 times, p1, yo, k2. 63 sts.

Row 30: S1 purlwise, purl to end.

Continuing in this manner, rep rows 1–8 of Feather Lace and AT SAME TIME increase the multiple of stitch repeats in brackets as work progresses for each new tier.

Continue until center spine of shawl, from cast on to triangle point, measures approximately 33"/84cm or to desired length, ending after Feather Lace row 8.

Left side Feather Tip bind offs

With RS facing, work first tier tip as follows:

Row 1: S1, k2tog, k6, k2tog, turn.
Row 2: P9, turn.
Row 3: S1, k2tog, k4, k2tog, turn.
Row 4: P7, turn.
Row 5: S1, k2tog, k2, k2tog, turn.
Row 6: P5, turn.
Row 7: S1, k2, k2tog, turn.
Row 8: P4, turn.
Row 9: S1, k1, k2tog, turn.
Row 10: P3, turn.
Row 11: S1, k2tog, psso, do not turn.

With RS facing, pick up knitwise and AT SAME TIME immediately bind off 10 sts evenly along decrease side. Knit 1 st (above a yarn over) from left needle and bind off. One st rem on right needle.

Work next and all rem left side Feather Tip bind offs to center spine as follows (with 1 st rem on right needle):

Row 1: K5, k2tog, turn.
Row 2: P7, turn.
Row 3: S1, k4, k2tog, turn.
Row 4: P6, turn.

Row 5: S1, k3, k2tog, turn.
Row 6: P5, turn.
Row 7: S1, k2, k2tog, turn.
Row 8: P4, turn.
Row 9: S1, k1, k2tog, turn.
Row 10: P3, turn.
Row 11: S1, k2tog, psso, do not turn.

With RS facing, pick up knitwise (see Glossary) and AT SAME TIME immediately bind off 10 sts evenly along decrease side. Knit 1 st (above a yarn over) from left needle and bind off. One st rem on right needle. Rep from * 28 more times (or to center section/point of triangle).

Center point

With 1 st rem on right needle:

Row 1: K8 (9 sts on right needle), turn.
Row 2: S1, p1, psso, p7, turn.
Row 3: S1, k1, psso, k6, turn.
Row 4: S1, p1, psso, p5, turn.
Row 5: S1, k1, psso, k4, turn.
Row 6: S1, p1, psso, p3, turn.
Row 7: S1, k1, psso, k2, turn.
Row 8: S1, p1, psso, p1, turn.
Row 9: K2tog. Cut yarn and pull tail through loop.

Right side Feather Tip bind offs

With WS facing, join yarn to top of triangle and work first tier tip as follows:

Row 1: S1, p2tog, p6, p2tog, turn.
Row 2: K9, turn.
Row 3: S1, p2tog, p4, p2tog, turn.
Row 4: K7, turn.
Row 5: S1, p2tog, p2, p2tog, turn.
Row 6: K5, turn.
Row 7: S1, p2, p2tog, turn.
Row 8: K4, turn.
Row 9: S1, p1, p2tog, turn.
Row 10: K3, turn.
Row 11: S1, p2tog, psso, do not turn.

With WS facing, pick up purlwise (see Glossary) and AT SAME TIME immediately bind off 10 sts evenly along decrease side. Purl 1 st (above a yarn over) from left needle and bind off. One st rem on right needle.

Work next and all rem right side Feather Tip bind offs as follows (with 1 st rem on right needle):

Row 1: P5, p2tog, turn.
Row 2: K7, turn.
Row 3: S1, p4, p2tog, turn.
Row 4: K6, turn.
Row 5: S1, p3, p2tog, turn.
Row 6: K5, turn.
Row 7: S1, p2, p2tog, turn.
Row 8: K4, turn.
Row 9: S1, p1, p2tog, turn.
Row 10: K3, turn.
Row 11: S1, p2tog, psso, do not turn.

With WS facing, pick up purlwise (see Glossary) and AT SAME TIME immediately bind off 10 sts evenly along decrease side. Purl 1 st (above a yarn over) from left needle and bind off. One st rem on right needle. . Rep from ** 28 more times (or to center section/point of triangle).

FINISHING

Darn ends. Wet block to desired measurements. For best results, use blocking wires and pins to stretch feather tips. After drying, it may also be necessary to iron tips flat to prevent curling. If tips still curl, just remember that feathers do ruffle...it's a fact of life.

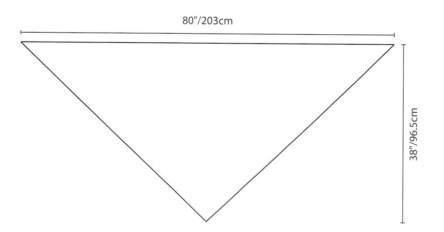

80"/203cm

38"/96.5cm

Chapter 7

Brokenhearted

his is the way she knew he was gone: The door was open. His boots were missing. The cage where he kept a hawk was empty. He'd never said a word. The night before he went missing he'd gathered the firewood, cleaned the pots, fed the hawk. He didn't bother to leave a note.

She ran out the door, barefoot, crying his name so loudly that all the birds in the trees rose up in one achingly blue cloud. She went to the edge of the lake and saw him on the other side. The water was black that day. His boat was on the shore directly across from her. The hawk was on his shoulder, but it flew back to her. The hawk, at least, was loyal. He, however, did not answer her calls. And he wasn't alone. There was a woman waiting for him. That was when her heart broke into two pieces that fell into the grass.

She went home, her heart in her hands. She kept her broken heart in a glass jar on her bedside table. In the dark, the glass glowed with pale red light. She shared her dinners with the hawk. Bones, turnips, onions, only bitter things. One night she dreamed the man who had left her told her he'd never really loved her. When she woke she took a knife and cut off her long gold hair. It was the part of her he'd always said he loved best. He'd insisted she wear it long, and she'd done as he asked, even though it was often tangled and difficult to comb. Now it was in a pile in a corner.

People started to talk about her, so she stayed away from town. Everyone knew she wasn't the same. If you looked at her carefully you could see the space where her heart should have been. It was empty, as if there was nothing more than a cloud in the place where her heart had been, the color a dim gray. To hide what she was missing, she took two sticks from the kindling, then reached for the pile of her own gold hair. She began to knit a vest so that no one could see what was missing inside her.

Without her heart she could no longer feel, and she was grateful for that. She had felt enough when she lost her heart beside the black lake. She worked in the garden in the hot sun all day long and was never tired. She stood knee-deep in the ice-cold lake to catch fish and didn't shiver. When she knitted her fingers never hurt even though the needles were made of splintering sticks. In the dark she curled up in bed to knit by the light of her own heart. Moths were drawn to the red light. But she felt nothing. Her heart was like a caged bird. It called to her, but she didn't answer.

The vest was done in no time. She wore it day and night so no one could tell how empty

53

she was. Then one day the hawk flew into the woods crying out and she followed. She found a man in the woods whose legs had been broken when he fell from a tree. She helped him home. When he leaned heavily on her, she didn't feel any pain. He was a carpenter who'd been looking for wood to fashion into tables and chairs. She let him sleep on her porch, and she didn't feel a thing when he thanked her and took her hand in his.

But the pieces of her heart encased in glass burned even more brightly through the night.

The doctor came and set the carpenter's legs and said he couldn't walk for four months. He would be a burden, but she didn't mind. She had no heart; she didn't care about anything, not how handsome he was, or how kind. When the hawk ate from his hand, not their usual bitter fare but sweet berries, the carpenter said nothing should be kept in a cage. She thought of her heart, that bird in a glass cage. She shrugged. Why should she care?

The carpenter ate supper with her, and in the evenings he set to work on carving a beautiful wooden bowl as a gift for all of her generosity. He fell in love with her when the snow began to fall.

I wouldn't do that if I were you, she told him. She showed him her heart in its glass container. She said it could never be put back together. But he was a carpenter, used to fixing things. He shook his head and smiled. He vowed he'd find a way.

Impossible, she said. The carpenter's legs were now healed enough for him to leave. *Go before I wake in the morning. Don't say goodbye.*

Instead he stayed awake all night. He'd often watched her knit in the evenings, and now he took up the needles. In the morning she saw what he'd done. He'd cut off all of his hair and used the strands to knit a pocket on her vest. Into that he'd placed the pieces of her heart. The longer she wore her heart in the pocket, the more it mended, until one day it was a whole heart, inside her once more. She still wears that vest, even though she's a married woman now, and her husband knows all there is to know about her heart. He gave it back to her, and no matter what happens, she doesn't intend to let go of it again.

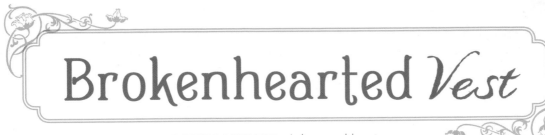

Brokenhearted Vest

DIFFICULTY: Advanced beginner

MATERIALS

Long Island Yarn & Farm (100yd/91m, 1.75oz/50g) 75% Llama, 25% Merino, 10 (12, 14) skeins in color Naturally Dyed with Cutch (A), 1 (2, 2) skeins in color Dirty Wash Denim (B).
Or any worsted-weight yarn that meets gauge.

Size 9 (5.5mm) needles or size to obtain gauge.

Cable needle.

Stitch holders.

Additional needle for 3-needle bind off.

Darning needle.

SIZES

Small (Medium, Large).

FINISHED MEASUREMENTS

40 (44, 48)"/101.5 (111.5, 122)cm hip width, 23 (23, 24½)"/58.5 (58.5, 62)cm length.

GAUGE

16 sts x 19 rows = 4"/10cm in K1, P1 Rib, after blocking.
18 sts x 21 rows = 4"/10cm in Climbing Cables stitch, after blocking.
Take time to check your gauge.

Knitting Wisdom

+ Selvedge stitches are extra stitches that are included for seaming. They are added to the lower sections of the vest. After the first bind offs, the selvedge stitches are removed.

+ This is a good pattern to learn how to cable without using a cable needle, by repositioning the stitches and then knitting them in a new order to create a cable. For the 3/3 LC: Put right needle behind work and slip into the back legs of the fourth, fifth, and sixth stitches; pull left needle from all 6 stitches (3 remain on right needle, 3 will drop toward front); insert left needle into the 3 open dropped stitches; slip 3 stitches from right needle back to left needle. Stitches have been repositioned. Knit across 6 stitches.

+ For the 3/3 RC: Put right needle to front of work and slip into the front legs of the fourth, fifth, and sixth stitches; pull left needle from all 6 stitches (3 remain on right needle, 3 will drop to back); insert left needle into the 3 open dropped stitches; slip 3 stitches from right back to left needle. Stitches have been repositioned. Knit across 6 stitches.

STITCH GUIDE

K1, P1 Rib (over an odd number of sts)
Row 1 (RS): K1, *p1, k1; rep from * to end.
Row 2 (WS): P1, *k1, p1; rep from * to end.

Climbing Cables (multiple of 16 + 8) for sizes small and large only
Row 1 (RS): *P1, k6, p2, k6, p1; rep from * to last 8 sts, p1, k6, p1.
Row 2 and all WS rows: *K1, p6, k2, p6, k1; rep from * to last 8 sts, k1, p6, k1.
Row 3: Rep row 1.
Row 5: *P1, 3/3 LC, p2, 3/3 RC, p1; rep from * to last 8 sts, p1, 3/3 LC, p1.
Rows 7, 9, and 11: Rep row 1.
Row 13: *P1, 3/3 RC, p2, 3/3 LC, p1; rep from * to last 8 sts, p1, 3/3 RC, p1.
Row 15: Rep row 1.
Row 16: Rep row 2.

Climbing Cables (multiple of 16) for size medium only
Row 1 (RS): *P1, k6, p2, k6, p1; rep from * to end.

Row 2 and all WS rows: *K1, p6, k2, p6, k1; rep from * to end.
Row 3: Rep row 1.
Row 5: *P1, 3/3 LC, p2, 3/3 RC, p1; rep from * to end.
Rows 7, 9, and 11: Rep row 1.
Row 13: *P1, 3/3 RC, p2, 3/3 LC, p1; rep from * to end.
Row 15: Rep row 1.
Row 16: Rep row 2.

3/3 LC (3 Over 3 Left Cross)
Slip 3 sts to cable needle, hold to front, k3, k3 from cable needle.

3/3 RC (3 Over 3 Right Cross)
Slip 3 sts to cable needle, hold to back, k3, k3 from cable needle.

For more abbreviations, stitches, and techniques, see Glossary.

INSTRUCTIONS

Back
With A, cast on 89 (97, 105) sts. Work in K1, P1 Rib for 5 rows, increasing 1 st on last row. 90 (98, 106) sts.
Row 1 (RS): K1 (selv st), pm, work row 1 of Climbing Cables to last st, pm, k1 (selv st).
Row 2 (WS): K1 (selv st), sm, work row 2 of Climbing Cables to last st, sm, k1 (selv st).
Continue in patterns as established until rows 1–16 of Climbing Cables have been worked 2 (3, 3) times, then work rows 1–8 of Climbing Cables 1 (0, 0) more time(s). Work measures approximately 8½ (10, 10)"/21.5 (25.5, 25.5)cm from cast on.
Bind off 18 sts at beg of next 2 rows.
Continue in pattern as established on rem 54 (62, 70) sts until piece measures approximately 23 (23, 24½)"/58.5 (58.5, 62)cm from cast on, ending with cable pattern row 8 or 16. On separate holders, place 14 (14, 16) sts for right shoulder, 26 (34, 38) sts for back neck, and 14 (14, 16) sts for left shoulder.

Front
With A, cast on 85 (93, 101) sts. Work in K1, P1 Rib for 5 rows. Begin cable and rib patterns on next row as follows:
Row 1 (RS): K1 (selv st), pm, work row 1 of Climbing Cables over next 24 sts, pm, p1, [k1, p1] 17 (21, 25) times, pm, work row 1 of Climbing Cables over next 24 sts, pm, k1 (selv st).
Row 2 (WS): K1 (selv st), sm, work row 2 of Climbing Cables over next 24 sts, pm, k1, [p1, k1] 17 (21, 25) times, sm, work row 2 of Climbing Cables over next 24 sts, sm, k1 (selv st).

Continue in patterns as established until rows 1–16 of Climbing Cables have been worked 2 (3, 3) times, then work rows 1–8 of Climbing Cables 1 (0, 0) more time(s). Bind off 18 sts at beg of next 2 rows.

Continue in patterns as established on rem 49 (57, 65) sts until piece measures 20 (20, 21½)"/51 (51, 54.5)cm from cast on.

Divide fronts for neck shaping on next RS row as follows: Work 24 (28, 34) sts, bind off 1, work to end. Working right and left fronts at same time with separate balls of yarn, continue in patterns as established until piece measures same as back, ending with cable pattern row 8 or 16. On separate holders, place 14 (14, 16) sts for each shoulder and 10 (14, 18) sts at each front for neck. Return held shoulder sts to needles and, with right sides together, join shoulders with 3-needle bind off.

Neck

Return held neck sts to one needle as follows: 10 (14, 18) held right neck sts, 26 (34, 38) held back neck sts, 10 (14, 18) held left neck sts = 46 (62, 74) sts. With RS facing, join A and work as follows: [P1, k1] 5 (7, 8) times, p2tog, then continue in K1, P1 Rib to end—45 (61, 69) sts. Work even as established in rib for 5½"/14cm. Bind off loosely in pattern.

Pocket

With B, cast on 40 (48, 56) sts. Work in K1, P1 Rib for 5 rows. Begin cable pattern on next row as follows:

Row 1 (RS): K1, *k6, p2; rep from * to last 7 sts, k7.
Row 2 and all WS rows: K1, *p6, k2; rep from * to last 7 sts, p6, k1.
Row 3: Rep row 1.

For sizes small and large only
Row 5: K1, *3/3 LC, p2, 3/3 RC, p2; rep from * to last 7 sts, 3/3 LC, k1.
Rows 7, 9, and 11: Rep row 1.
Row 13: K1, *3/3 RC, p2, 3/3 LC, p2; rep from * to last 7 sts, 3/3 RC, k1.

For size medium only
Row 5: K1, *3/3 LC, p2, 3/3 RC, p2; rep from * to last 15 sts, 3/3 LC, p2, 3/3 RC, k1.
Rows 7, 9, and 11: Rep row 1.
Row 13: K1, *3/3 RC, p2, 3/3 LC, p2; rep from * to last 15 sts, 3/3 RC, p2, 3/3 LC, k1.

For all sizes
Row 15: Rep row 1.
Row 16: Rep row 2.
Rep rows 1–16 once more, then rows 1–8 once.

FINISHING

Seam sides. Attach pocket to lower front on center rib panel with opening at top. Darn ends. Steam or block to desired measurements.

Climbing Cables Chart: Sizes Small and Large

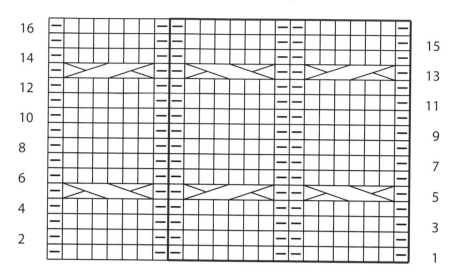

Climbing Cables Chart: Size Medium

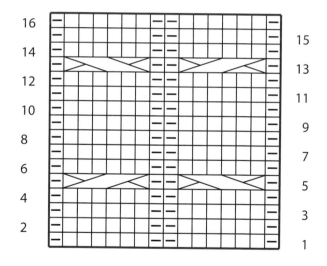

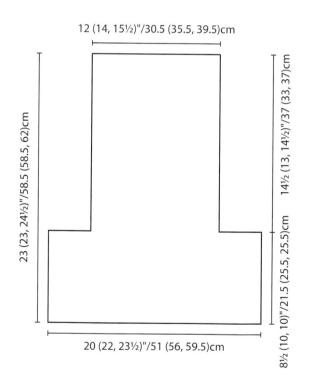

12 (14, 15½)"/30.5 (35.5, 39.5)cm

23 (23, 24½)"/58.5 (58.5, 62)cm

14½ (13, 14½)"/37 (33, 37)cm

8½ (10, 10)"/21.5 (25.5, 25.5)cm

20 (22, 23½)"/51 (56, 59.5)cm

Climbing Cables Chart Key

☐ K on RS, P on WS

⊟ P on RS, K on WS

 3/3 RC

▨ 3/3 LC

☐ Repeat

Chapter 8

Charm

She loved him from the time she first saw him, but he never noticed her. She was a plain young woman with dark eyes who didn't speak up for herself. But she knew what she wanted and she knew what she felt.

She had been walking in the woods and there he was. They might have passed each other in the city a hundred times without noticing each other, but now her eyes were open. She crouched down behind a tree so she could watch him, the way a person might observe a rare creature. For this was the thing that made her love him: He was kind.

There was a blue jay caught in a hunter's snare. The young man climbed a tree and carefully freed the bird from the netting. When the jay flew away, her heart flew with it. In a show of gratitude, the jay returned to sit on the man's shoulder, and the young woman found that she was jealous, and wished she could sing as sweetly into his ear.

Other men were invisible, nothing more than shadows. Often she spied the man she loved among the crowds of the city, but he never looked her way. She wanted to speak to him, and followed behind, ready to declare herself, but no words came out. She went to the printer's shop where he worked, but she found herself unable to walk through the door. She was mute in his presence. For what she felt, words would never be enough.

She saw him at dances, with other women who weren't afraid to speak up. She decided then that her shyness was a curse, one she must be rid of. In the end, she did what her mother and her grandmother and all her aunts had told her she must never do.

She went to the witch.

The cottage was in a far field surrounded by stones, and could only be found by those in need. When the young woman arrived, the witch was on her porch, knitting.

What have you brought me? the witch asked.

Luckily, the young woman had a new strand of blue beads the color of the sky, which she presented as an offering. The witch tapped at them, knowing they were made of clay rather than precious stones. All the same she slipped them on and listened to the young woman's story, then she told the lovestruck woman what she must do.

Catch a blue jay, pluck out its heart, and boil it into a tea to give to the man you love. If you can't do that, maybe you don't deserve his love.

The young woman returned to town, running all the way home. She saw jays in the trees and she knew she could never be that cruel.

Still, she couldn't give up. She went back to the witch the next day. Again, the witch was knitting. This time the young woman brought her a pie made from the apples of the tree in the center of town, the one that was said to bring good fortune. The witch shrugged, unimpressed, though she ate every crumb. Then she advised her visitor.

Make a tea of your own blood and his, and then both drink from the very same cup.

Again, the remedy was impossible. She could not even speak to the man she loved; how could she draw his blood, and why would she ever want to hurt him so?

On the third visit she brought yarn spun from the finest wool. The witch nodded and stopped her knitting. At last she was pleased. She handed the wool back to the young woman. Now she gave the best advice of all.

Knit three small bags. Fill each with every plant that grows in the place where you first spied him, then for three nights place a sachet outside his window.

The young woman followed the witch's instructions. She knitted all through the night, three bags perfect for gathering herbs, but in the morning, when she went into the woods, she couldn't find the spot where she'd first spied the man. She wandered through the fields, desperate. Late in the day, she saw the blue jay in the treetops. She followed him until she recognized the very place where she had lost her heart. She gathered lavender, wild roses, ferns, wild mint. When the bags were full, she went to her beloved's house and placed one beneath his open bedroom window, as the witch had instructed. She did so the next night, and the night after that.

Each night he dreamed of the scent of mint and lavender and roses and ferns, and each day he searched out that fragrance. He thought about little else. In time he couldn't sleep. People who knew him joked that he must have fallen in love, and he agreed, but who his beloved was remained a mystery. He followed the scent of the perfume into the marketplace each day, and just when he thought love was nothing more than a dream, there she was, waiting for him, the woman who was meant for him all along.

૨ঌ

Charm *Bags*

DIFFICULTY: Beginner

MATERIALS

Shibui Knits Rain (135yd/123m, 50g/1.75oz) 100% Cotton, 1 skein each in colors #2003 Ash, #2022 Mineral, #2035 Fog for bags, 1 skein in color #2004 Ivory for I-cord handle.
Or any DK-weight yarn (see Knitting Wisdom) that meets gauge.

Size 6 (4.0mm) needles or size to obtain gauge.

Size 6 (4.0mm) double-point needles for I-cord.

Darning needle.

Crochet hook (optional, for threading I-cord through top of bag).

SIZES

One size.

FINISHED MEASUREMENTS

5"/12.5cm width, 4¼"/11cm length.

GAUGE

22 sts x 30 rows = 4"/10cm in Stockinette stitch.
Take time to check your gauge.

Knitting Wisdom

✦ Each bag uses approximately 65yd/60m of one color yarn aside from the contrast color for I-cord handle. A traditional 50g skein or ball of DK-weight yarn will yield at least 2 bags at this gauge.

✦ For a crisp fabric, use a cotton, linen, or hemp fiber. A rough and more natural wool, such as a Shetland or Icelandic, would also work well with this piece. A local farm yarn that may still have some hay stuck in it suits the theme of plants and nature from the story.

✦ Fill these bags with lavender to make beautiful sachets, use them to store precious jewelry for safekeeping, or use one as a small wallet for your loose change.

✦ Use ribbon or twine as an alternative to the I-cord if you are not familiar with the technique.

STITCH GUIDE

Garter stitch
Knit every row.

Stockinette stitch
Row 1 (RS): Knit.
Row 2 (WS): Purl.

For more abbreviations, stitches, and techniques, see Glossary.

INSTRUCTIONS

Using yarn in your choice of bag color, cast on 32 sts. Work in Garter stitch for 8 rows. Change to Stockinette stitch and work for 46 rows or until piece measures approximately 7"/18cm, end after a RS row. Change back to Garter stitch and work for 19 rows or until piece measures approximately 8¾"/22cm from cast on. Bind off on next WS row.
Using yarn in your choice of cord color, make a 19"/48cm I-cord.

FINISHING

Fold piece in half along fold line (see schematic). Seam sides, leaving top open at cast-on/bound-off edges. Darn ends. Block or steam lightly to measurements. Use a darning needle or crochet hook to weave the I-cord in and out along the top edge (between the top 2 garter ridges, approximately every 3–4 sts). Sew the I-cord ends together to form a circle.

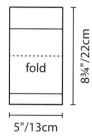

fold

8¾"/22cm

5"/13cm

Chapter 9

Rose

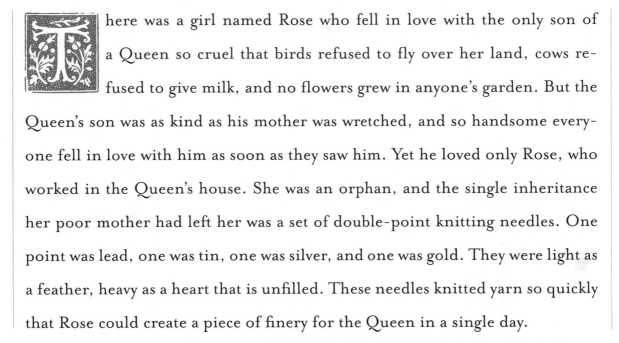

There was a girl named Rose who fell in love with the only son of a Queen so cruel that birds refused to fly over her land, cows refused to give milk, and no flowers grew in anyone's garden. But the Queen's son was as kind as his mother was wretched, and so handsome everyone fell in love with him as soon as they saw him. Yet he loved only Rose, who worked in the Queen's house. She was an orphan, and the single inheritance her poor mother had left her was a set of double-point knitting needles. One point was lead, one was tin, one was silver, and one was gold. They were light as a feather, heavy as a heart that is unfilled. These needles knitted yarn so quickly that Rose could create a piece of finery for the Queen in a single day.

Everything she made for the Queen brought a thousand compliments, and the Queen was satisfied with her, for Rose never once made an error. Then one day the son of the Queen came to sit with Rose while she worked. When he told Rose of his love for her she dropped a stitch as she knitted glovelettes for the Queen. She dropped another when he kissed her and a third when he said they should run away together. Without thinking, Rose allowed the guard to collect the glovelettes to bring to the Queen. She forgot her mistakes until she was called to the throne room.

As soon as the Queen heard of her son's love for her servant, she went to a magician, who took note of the dropped stitches and placed an unraveling spell on the glovelettes. Now the Queen had only unstitched yarn around her wrists. She said Rose had plotted to tie her up and steal her son by the means of magic. Rose was led to a tower where four locks were set upon the door. No matter what the Queen's son did, no matter how many keys he had the locksmiths make, he could not open these latches. At last he went to his mother and begged for another chance for his beloved Rose: If she could make perfect glovelettes, would the Queen set her free? He begged and pleaded until at last the Queen agreed. But she used the situation to her advantage.

But if the girl manages to do so, and if she's released, she must leave this land at once. She can never return.

Her son had little choice but to agree, but he, too, used their pact to suit himself.

If she leaves, I go with her. That is our bargain.

The Queen was unhappy with their bargain, but she told those closest to her that no agreement is set in stone, especially one that is made of yarn.

Rose was given white yarn, the color of snow. Before the door was closed, a boy brought her a bouquet of white roses. They were the only roses that grew in this country, hidden in the Queen's courtyard. The Queen's son had sent them to remind Rose of his love for her. Rose set to work knitting by moonlight, by sunlight, and by shadow. Because flowers could not bloom long in this country, rose petals soon littered the stone floor. To honor her love for the Queen's son, Rose knitted the petals into her work until each glovelette was marked with a flower.

When she was done, she was brought back to the royal chambers. The Queen carefully examined the glovelettes. There was not a single mistake. Or so it seemed, for those who look for an error can always invent one.

I didn't want white! the Queen declared. *I wanted red.* She threw the glovelettes on the ground. *These are worthless.*

But the roses the Queen's son had sent to his beloved had been enchanted by his love, and when the Queen's maid went to retrieve the glovelettes and held them up, all there were amazed. The roses had the ability to change color, and when the glovelettes were turned inside out, they were red.

Rose was rushed back to the tower and the four locks were bolted, even though the Queen's wish had been fulfilled. It was now said that she was an enchantress, and perhaps she was. She still had the knitting needles her mother had given her, her most precious possession. All at once she knew what she must do in order to free herself. She unlocked the latches with the needles: lead for lead, tin for tin, silver for silver, gold for gold. She ran down the stairs and into the Queen's garden, where the Queen's son was waiting for her. When they left they took the rose tree that turned from white to red with them, and in their new country all of the roses were enchanted and you never knew from day to day what color they would be, but you knew they would be beautiful, and that was more than enough.

Rose *Glovelettes*

DIFFICULTY: Advanced

MATERIALS

Stacy Charles Fine Yarns Julie (125yd/115m, 1.75oz/50g) 75% Extra-fine Merino Wool, 25% Silk, 2 skeins: 1 each in colors #09 Pearl [A] and #11 Ruby [B].
Or approximately 72yd/66m of any sport-weight yarn that meets gauge in each of 2 contrast colors.

Size 4 (3.5mm) double-point needles.

Size 3 (3.25mm) double-point needles or size to obtain gauge.

Darning needle.

SIZES

One size fits most.

FINISHED MEASUREMENTS

8"/20.5cm circumference, 7½"/19cm length.

GAUGE

45 sts x 32 rows = 4"/10cm in Double Knitting with smaller needles, after blocking.
Take time to check your gauge.

Knitting Wisdom

✦ Julie by Stacy Charles Fine Yarns used in these glovelettes is marked as a DK weight, though when knit tightly for this technique, the silk and wool blend fiber gets the correct gauge. An alternate fiber should be a sport-weight yarn, and it is important to check gauge in rounds.

✦ These glovelettes are worked in rounds using four double-point needles in the double-knitting technique, except for the thumbhole, where rows are worked flat. You may vary the method to use 2 circulars or Magic Loop. If desired, these glovelettes can be worked flat and seamed, leaving a thumbhole opening.

✦ In double knitting, both sides of a fabric are worked simultaneously. By working knit stitches with color A and purl stitches with color B, a fabric is created that has Stockinette facing on both the front and back sides, with the colors reversed. The color not in use is carried in front or in back of slipped stitches to lie stranded between the stitches. Pull tightly between stitches in any one color, staying on right side or wrong side of work. In contrast to Fair Isle knitting, there is no need to have loose stranding behind the alternate color, as the stitches,

though alternated on needles while working, will eventually separate to create 2 front-facing sides.

✦ In Solid Double Knitting, one color of work is facing and the contrast color is on the reverse side without any pattern. Right side of work is color A facing; wrong side of work is color B facing. The sides of the fabric will not meet, and a space is left between them. When working a pattern such as the Rose Chart and Dot Pattern, the stitches cross, and the sides are joined.

✦ This pattern is written in my preferred method of working each color separately. The alternate method is to hold 2 strands and work both colors at the same time.

✦ For ease of reading the Rose Chart, instead of working whole rounds, I suggest working one color to the end of a needle, returning to the beginning of that needle, and working the second color before continuing to the next needle. The green line dividers on the chart show how the stitches are divided between 3 double-point needles. This method helps eliminate the need to undo many stitches if you notice a mistake.

With A and larger dpn, using long-tail method, cast on 45 sts. Divide evenly onto 3 dpns and join to work in rounds with knit side facing, being careful not to twist sts.

Increase on first round as follows: Holding A and B together, *k1 with A, do not drop st from left needle, p1 with B into front of same st, then drop cast-on st from left needle. Two sts (one of each color) made from one; rep to end. 90 sts.

Change to smaller dpns. The first st, with RS facing, will be color A.
Work Solid Double Knitting (working in rounds) for 10 rounds.

Begin Rose Chart
Following directions given in Rose Chart notes, work rounds 1–24 of Rose Chart.
Work 2 rounds in Solid Double Knitting (working in rounds).

Thumbhole
Work Solid Double Knitting (working flat) for 10 rows. With RS facing, work 1 more row (A and B), then join to work in rounds again.
Work 2 rounds in Solid Double Knitting (working in rounds), then work 1 round in Dot Pattern as follows: *With A, k1, s1 wyif, s1 wyib, p1, k1, s1 wyif; rep from * to end. **With B, s1 wyib, p1, k1, s1 wyif, s1 wyib, p1; rep from ** to end. Work Solid Double Knitting (working in rounds) for 10 more rounds.
With larger needle, bind off with color A by k2tog (1 A st and 1 B st) as you continue binding off to end.

FINISHING

Darn ends. Steam lightly to block.

STITCH GUIDE

Solid Double Knitting (working in rounds)
*Wyib, k1 with A, bring both yarns forward, slip next st (B) purlwise, bring both yarns to back; rep from * to end. Drop A, pick up B, being careful not to twist sts. **Wyib, slip next st (A) purlwise, bring both yarns to front, p1 with B, bring both yarns to back; rep from ** to end. Working each color once around equals 1 round worked.

Solid Double Knitting (working flat) for thumbhole
Using same method as Solid Double Knitting, with RS facing, work color A to end, then work color B to end. Turn glovelette inside out so WS is facing. Twist yarns to avoid a gap, work color B to end, then work color A to end. Turn glovelette inside out again, so RS is facing. Two rows worked.

For more abbreviations, stitches, and techniques, see Glossary.

Rose Chart

Each square of the chart represents the color facing and equals 2 stitches, a knit in the color facing, and a slipped stitch. Using my method, completing 1 round of A and 1 round of B equals 1 "row" of chart worked.

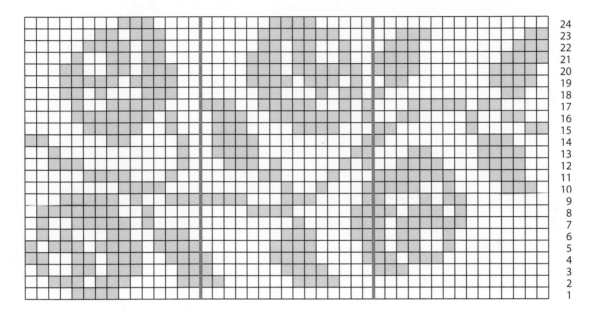

Rose Chart Key

☐ A

▨ B

☐ Switch to next dpn

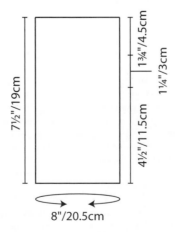

Chapter 10

River Girl

 he watched other girls from town walking through the meadow to the dance hall and she cried green tears. She was not like them. She was half fish, the half that made it impossible for her to walk through a meadow or dance all night long. Her tail was silver, and her eyes were, too, and there wasn't a more beautiful creature, or a sadder one, in all the world.

One night she spied a man, one so tall and handsome she couldn't look away from him. She watched him all summer as he cut across the fields. He caught sight of her once, and once was all it took. He saw her face as she peered at him from the riverside. *Who are you?* he cried, lovestruck. He tramped through the mud and made his way through the reeds. Without even thinking, he threw himself into the water, searching for her.

She sank down into the depths, terrified that he would see her for what she was: A freak, a monster, more of a fish than a girl. She could hold her breath for an hour, which was a good thing, because he searched until he was forced to give up. Waterlogged, thwarted, he perched on the riverbank. *Where are you?* he cried out, confused.

His friends came to look for him and dragged him home. Had they not, he would have still been searching when morning came.

Now more than ever she longed to be human. She began to waste away, her skin fading to a pale blue, her hair turning green at the edg-es. The scales of her tail scattered like discs of moonlight as she herself grew dim. He came back every day, but what would he want with a monster? She held her breath and waited for him to leave and then, when he was gone, she cried once more.

The fish took pity on her. They collected silver scales and wove them into stockings, knitting them together with water lilies and moonlight. When she slipped them on, she had legs. She climbed onto the shore and walked through the meadow. She was tipsy at first but soon grew stronger, joyous at all she could do. She ran down the road, and when she passed a farmhouse she borrowed a dress from a clothesline, pulled it on, then raced to the dance hall, amazed at how far her new legs could take her.

She stopped at the door. There in front of her was everything she had ever wanted. As soon as the man spied her, he knew her. They danced as if no one else existed, and for them no one did. But then her stockings began to unravel. Silver scales littered the floor. She ran away, as fast as her legs could take her, faster than she'd thought possible. Her tears left a green trail that led to the river, and the man who loved her dashed after her. He saw her slip off her stockings and dive back into the river.

So now he knew. But it didn't matter.

If anything, he wanted her more.

He went to his grandmother, who knew more about the world than anyone else. He showed her the silver stockings he'd gathered from the shore and told her of his love. His grandmother promised she could knit the stockings together and this time the change would last. The old woman went into the woods to collect lily of the valley, earthbound blooms to mix with the water lilies, along with sunshine to bind the moonlight. She set to knitting and she didn't stop until she had finished the stockings. Then she folded them carefully into her pocket and went down to the shoreline.

She had been here before, a long time ago. That was why she understood wanting something that belonged to the river. She'd longed for a grandson and had plucked a boy out of the river with her fishing net. He, too, was part fish until she made him socks that were knitted of the earthly elements, brambles and leaves and vines. She had raised him and loved him and now he was her own. If he wanted the River Girl, it made perfect sense. Who was she to say no?

The grandmother put her hand in the water and the girl came to gaze at her, curious.

If you wear these stockings, you can have what you want, the grandmother said. *But it has to be your heart's desire.*

The River Girl took her hand. *He is.*

When the River Girl followed the old woman back to town, there wasn't a happier person to be found. The old woman might know everything, but perhaps the girl knew a little more. You never lose who you really are. When she saw her beloved, she ran to him, and not long after, they married. They soon had a child, a little girl who was half fish. They called her Ella, for that was the grandmother's name. The grandmother was now so very old she could no longer knit. She told her grandson's wife what she needed, and the River Girl went to the forest to gather lily of the valley. But she also went to the river for a basket of water lilies. She knitted all night long.

Their little girl could run and dance and live a life like any other girl in town. But in the summertime when the grass was tall, they went back to the river in the evenings. They were a family after all, and they knew where they came from. They removed their stockings before they waded in. They knew that all things are possible when you're true to yourself. They swam along with the fish, but they never lost sight of the shore. They belonged to two worlds, and because of this their love was, and always would be, twice as strong.

River Girl Stockings

DIFFICULTY: Intermediate

MATERIALS

Stacy Charles Fine Yarns Stella (76.5yd/70m, 25g/0.88oz) 74% Silk, 26% Lurex Metallic, 4 balls in color #01 Silver Mist.
Or any worsted-weight yarn that meets gauge (see Knitting Wisdom).

Size 8 (5.0mm) needles or size to obtain gauge.

Size 6 (4.0mm) needles or 2 sizes smaller than larger needle.

Removable stitch marker or piece of contrast yarn.

Darning needle.

Approximately 3yd/2.75m of ⅝"/16mm ribbon, cut into 2 pieces.

Four decorative beads, approximately ¼"/6mm to ½"/12mm each.

SIZES

One size.

FINISHED MEASUREMENTS

Approximately 9"/23cm top circumference, 15¼"/38.5cm length. Will stretch to fit.

GAUGE

22 sts x 30 rows = 4"/10cm in Fishnet Lace stitch with larger needle, after blocking.
Take time to check your gauge.

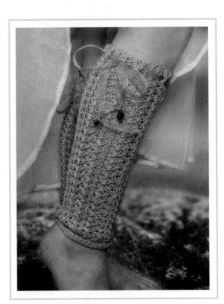

Knitting Wisdom

✦ The Lurex in Stella makes it a very stretchy fiber. If you choose a substitute yarn, make sure to use a comparable fiber.

✦ Stocking is written to be worked flat but can easily be worked in rounds to eliminate the seam by casting on 48 stitches, joining for rounds, and removing the purl stitch at end of row.

STITCH GUIDE

K1, P1 Rib (over an odd number of sts)
Row 1 (RS): P1, *k1, p1; rep from * to end.
Row 2 (WS): K1, *p1, k1; rep from * to end.

Stockinette stitch
Row 1 (RS): Knit.
Row 2 (WS): Purl.

Fishnet Lace (multiple of 8 + 1)
Row 1 (RS): *P1, yo, CDD, yo, k4; rep from * to last st, p1.
Row 2 (WS): K1, *p7, k1; rep from * to end.
Row 3: *P1, k4, yo, CDD (see Glossary), yo; rep from * to last st, p1.
Row 4: K1, *p7, k1; rep from * to end.

For more abbreviations, stitches, and techniques, see Glossary.

INSTRUCTIONS (MAKE 2)

With larger needle, loosely cast on 49 sts. Work K1, P1 Rib for 4 rows. Change to Fishnet Lace and work until piece measures 10"/25.5cm from cast on.
Change to smaller needle on next row, placing a removable stitch marker or a contrast yarn on this row to mark the change of gauge. Continue in Fishnet Lace for 4"/10cm from marker, end after a WS row.
Change to Stockinette stitch and decrease on next RS row as follows: K1, *k2tog, k2; rep from * to end. 37 sts.
Next row (WS): Purl.
Continue in Stockinette stitch for 1¼"/3cm. Bind off loosely.

FINISHING

Fold piece in half along fold line (see schematic) and seam. Darn ends. Block lightly by steaming. Weave ribbon in and out of the yarn overs in first pattern row of Fishnet Lace (behind the CDDs). Tie loosely and trim if needed to hang at desired length. Slip a bead onto a ribbon end, about 2"/5cm up, and tie a knot to keep it in place. Rep at other ribbon end.

Fishnet Lace Chart

Fishnet Lace Chart Key

- ☐ K on RS, P on WS
- ⊟ P on RS, K on WS
- ⊼ CDD (see Glossary)
- ⊙ YO
- ☐ Repeat

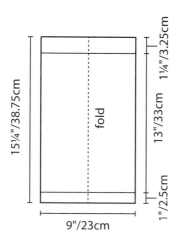

Chapter 11
Feather

She lived in the woods where there were only brambles and it was almost impossible to see the sky. No one had entered or left these woods since the time she was stolen from her parents. She didn't remember that day. She'd been brought here to be a maid for the oldest woman who had ever lived. When the girl was little more than a baby she was set to work scrubbing pots and pans. At the age of five she cooked the old lady's food. At six she learned how to spin yarn, and at seven she learned how to knit. She never received a compliment or a kind word. But now she was grown, nearly a woman. She stood at the window. She watched the birds that flew overhead and knew she could stay no longer.

It's time for me to leave, the girl told the old woman one day. *I've helped you all I can. Now I'll have my own life.*

The old woman shrugged. She often spoke in riddles. *You'll be able to leave on the day you can fly like a bird.*

It seemed an impossible task, but the girl knew it was a puzzle, and she was determined to solve it.

Each evening, after the old woman fell asleep, the girl climbed out the window and sat on the roof. From here she could see through the brambles to the stars above, and when she saw a falling star she made her wish. Freedom and flight were what she wanted, and the start of a new life.

The following day a bluebird came to the window and left a hundred blue feathers. Right away she spun them into thread. The yarn was the deepest blue that had ever been seen, so bright it was as if she held sapphires in her hands. She made certain to hide the ball of yarn beneath her pillow.

The next evening she wished on another star. The following morning a cardinal came and left two hundred red feathers. She spun these into thread while the old woman was sleeping. It was the color of rubies. Under her pillow it went.

She made her third wish on a falling star, and in the morning a goldfinch came and left her three hundred gold feathers. Again the girl spun them into thread. Anyone who saw the yarn would have thought it was real gold. This she hid beneath two pillows, for the yarn was aglow, as if she'd captured a slice of the sun.

From then on the girl spent the nights knitting a hat that was blue as the sky, red as rubies, gold as priceless metal, and soft as feathers to the touch. As she worked she thought of freedom and clear skies. In the morning she slipped on the hat, and to her great surprise she rose up from the floor. She felt light-headed, but sure of herself.

When she went to show the old woman that she had completed the task, they both knew nothing could keep her grounded anymore.

The old woman was now a hundred and ten years old. On this morning she cried for the first time in her life. *I should have been kinder,* she said, *but I didn't know how to be. I myself was brought here when I was five years old, and the old lady who raised me was even crueler than I've been. I have wasted a hundred and five years in the land of cruelty, and all I ask is that my last day be spent in freedom.*

The girl considered. She might lose one more day, but if she didn't practice kindness, she, too, might become an old woman with regrets. That night, when the moon rose, the girl helped the old woman into a cart. She pulled the cart along the rutted road even though she knew she could fly. When they reached a meadow they stopped and watched the sun rise. There were thousands of birds in the sky. The old woman handed the girl a bag filled with sapphires and rubies and gold so that she might make her own way in the world.

She whispered her gratitude for the gift of this last, glorious day.

That night the girl buried the old woman in a field. There were no brambles, for all the brambles had disappeared as if they had never grown in these woods. At last the girl could see the path that led to the city and the rest of her life. She went as the birds fly, and because of this, she was there in no time at all.

Feather Hat

DIFFICULTY: Advanced beginner

MATERIALS

Dragonfly Fibers Damsel
(335yd/306m, 4oz/113g) 100%
Superwash Merino Wool, 1 skein
in color Sugar Shack.
*Or approximately 200yd/183m of
any sport-weight yarn that meets
gauge.*

Size 4 (3.5mm) needles.

Size 6 (4.0mm) 16"/40cm circular
needles or size to obtain gauge.

Size 2 (2.75mm) double-point
needles for I-cord.

Stitch marker.

Darning needle.

SIZES

Small/Medium (Large).

FINISHED MEASUREMENTS

16 (19½)"/40.5 (49.5)cm circumference, 10"/25cm length.

GAUGE

23 sts x 30 rounds = 4"/10cm in
Feather and Fan stitch on largest
needle, after blocking.
23 sts x 32 rounds = 4"/10cm in
Stockinette stitch on largest needle.
Take time to check your gauge.

Knitting Wisdom

- ✦ The first size has negative ease and will stretch to fit a youth or a woman's medium-sized head comfortably. If you prefer a slouchier hat, work the larger size.

- ✦ The Twisted Rib band is knit flat, and the knit stitch is twisted in every row. If worked in rounds, every other row in ribbing will have purls worked through the back loops.

- ✦ Knit a simpler version of this hat by omitting the I-cord. Simply seam the sides of the ribbing together to finish.

- ✦ With the larger size, note that 1 less stitch is increased than with the smaller for correct multiples to work the Feather and Fan pattern.

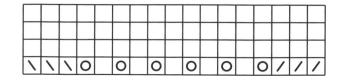

4
3
2
1

STITCH GUIDE

Twisted Rib (worked flat over an odd number of sts)
Row 1 (RS): *K1tbl, p1; rep from * to last st, k1tbl.
Row 2 (WS): P1, *k1tbl, p1; rep from * to end.

Feather and Fan (worked in the round over a multiple of 17 sts)
Round 1: *[K2tog] 3 times, [yo, k1] 5 times, yo, [ssk] 3 times; rep from * to end.
Rounds 2, 3, and 4: Knit.

For more abbreviations, stitches, and techniques, see Glossary.

Feather and Fan Chart Key

- ☐ K
- ☑ K2tog
- ☒ SSK
- ☉ YO

INSTRUCTIONS

With size 4 (3.5mm) needle, cast on 95 (113) sts. Work flat in Twisted Rib pattern for 12 rows.
Change to size 6 (4.0mm) needle. Increase on next RS row as follows: K5, [M1, k14] 6 times, M1 (0), k6. 102 (119) sts. Place marker and join to work in rounds, being careful not to twist sts. Knit 1 round.
Work in Feather and Fan pattern until piece measures 10"/25.5cm from cast on, end after round 4. Cut yarn, leaving a generous tail. With darning needle, thread tail through rem sts and gather to close top. Darn ends.

FINISHING

With dpns, cast on 3 sts and work I-cord for approximately 12"/30.5cm (see Glossary). Thread or lace the cord through sides of ribbing. Knot ends of I-cord, then tie or knot together.

Twisted Rib Chart

2

1

Twisted Rib Chart Key

☐ K on RS, P on WS

⊟ P on RS

⊍ K1tbl on RS and WS

☐ Repeat

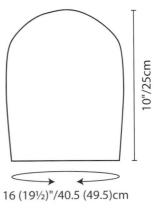

10"/25cm

16 (19½)"/40.5 (49.5)cm

Chapter 12

The Night of the Witch

 very few years they came searching, and this was the year they found them. Three sisters living at the edge of the forest. The youngest sister was at the river when it happened. She had long black hair and ember eyes and was so quiet it sometimes seemed she could disappear into the night. She knew something was wrong because the fish stopped swimming and birds fell from the sky. She felt whatever her sisters felt, but because she was the youngest, she felt even more. She felt a surge of fear beneath her skin. She had the sense that she had been torn from home, wrapped in chains, thrown into a dungeon. She ran as fast as she could, but it was too late. The witch hunters had come and gone. Her sisters had been taken to the city. There they were trapped in a jail cell whose lock had no key.

The youngest sister had always taken her sisters' advice; now she had no choice but to make her own decisions. She packed her bag and set off through the woods. She took what she thought she might need: a black dress, her knitting needles, a loaf of bread, a mirror. Halfway to the city she came to the house of the oldest witch, one who was so wise she had never been caught. In exchange for the wise woman's help, the youngest sister gave her the mirror. Whoever looked in the glass would see herself as she was when she was young. Pleased by this vision, the wise woman gave the youngest sister instructions. She was to take pieces of the night and knit them into long gloves before she went through the city gates. *They'll be your map,* the wise woman said. *Walk where the night leads you and you will never be found.*

The youngest sister did as she was told. When she climbed the tallest tree she still couldn't reach the sky, so she tossed bread crumbs to the ravens. They came to her with strands of night attached to their talons. Then and there she began to knit the inky black night yarn. It was so dark no one could see the gloves she had made, for she was knitting pure midnight. When she was done, she pulled on the gloves and set off for the city gates. She heard the guards say the witches were kept underground, in a cage without a key. They didn't notice when she slipped past. In her black dress, with her long black hair, and her night gloves, she was nothing more than a shadow.

She knew what she needed. Quickly, she found her way to the locksmith's house. She knocked on the door even though it was the middle of the night. He was tall and handsome and kindhearted, but his eyes could not tolerate full sun. Because of this he worked at night. This was the reason he opened the door, and the reason he saw her for who she was, a woman as beautiful as the night sky.

She needed a key that would open any door, just as she had opened his heart. She waited by the fire while he worked on the perfect key, a simple form made of silver, the one metal a witch can tolerate. He told her that if she didn't come back he would find her. In exchange for the key he had made, she left him the key to the house in the woods, made of a raven's feather.

To find her sisters she unwound the gloves. The unspooled black yarn cast itself along the street. She followed the path of the yarn as if it were a map. No one could see her, not even the witch hunters celebrating in the center of town, for wherever the night yarn led it was as dark as midnight. She went into the prison and down six flights of steps. The last of the yarn stopped in front of the cell that had no key. Her two sisters were waiting for her, the one with pale hair who looked like moonlight, and the one with bright hair who looked like a star. They had been crying and a pool had formed, so deep they would soon drown in their own tears. The youngest sister hurried. She slipped the locksmith's key into the lock and the door fell open.

The three sisters quickly retraced the path of the night yarn, gathering it as they went. The silver key was melting in the youngest sister's hand, turning into a silver ring. The locksmith had fashioned it that way so she wouldn't forget him. She felt her heart tugged upon when she thought of the locksmith, but she couldn't stay. Still, she couldn't quite let him go.

As they were escaping the city, the youngest sister let the ball of yarn fall to the ground. It unwound as she fled, creating a path to their door. You had to be acquainted with the night to see the path it made, but the locksmith had no problem seeing in the darkest part of the woods, even at the darkest hour of the night. He saw ravens sleeping in the trees and black roses blooming. When he got to the witches' house, he used the midnight yarn to surround it so that no witch hunter would ever find it again. Anyone passing by would see only the color of the night. Then he used the key the youngest sister had given him. He never went back to the city after that. From then on he preferred to climb to the top of the tallest tree with his beloved and watch the darkness fall down around them, as they counted the stars in the sky.

Witch Gloves

DIFFICULTY: Intermediate

MATERIALS

String Angel (136yd/125m, 50g/1.75oz) 100% Silk, 2 balls in color #67 Ebony (A).
Or approximately 270yd/246m of any sport-weight yarn that meets gauge.

Stacy Charles Fine Yarns Celine (163yd/149m, 20g/0.7oz) 60% Viscose, 40% Sinflex Polyester Metallic, 1 ball in color #11 Black Gold (B).
Or approximately 50yd/46m of any lace-weight yarn that meets gauge.

Size 5 (3.75mm) needles or size to obtain gauge.

Size 7 (4.5mm) needles.

Split ring or locking stitch markers or small amount of contrast yarn.

Darning needle.

SIZES

One size fits most.

FINISHED MEASUREMENTS

16"/41cm length, 6"/15cm circumference. Stretches to fit most arm widths.

GAUGE

22 sts x 32 rows = 4"/10cm in Stockinette stitch with A on smaller needle, after blocking.
Take time to check your gauge.

Knitting Wisdom

- ✦ Gloves are knit flat and seamed. They are designed this way because it is more manageable for the lace as well as the increase of stitches for the ruffled cuff.

- ✦ Working with size 7 (4.5mm) needles on sport-weight yarn makes these gloves comfortable and stretchy.

- ✦ When working stripes, carry yarn B up when not in use; do not cut yarn until all stripes are completed.

- ✦ To note placement of thumb gusset for finishing, use a split ring or locking stitch marker on the bar between 2 stitches of the knitted fabric, as directed in the pattern (ppm), when working the ruffle.

STITCH GUIDE

K1, P1 Rib (over an odd number of sts)
Row 1 (RS): K1, *p1, k1; rep from * to end.
Row 2 (WS): P1, *k1, p1; rep from * to end.

Witchy Lace (multiple of 9 + 2)
Row 1 (RS): K1, *k3, yo, CDD, yo, k3; rep from * to last st, k1.
Row 2 and all WS rows: Purl.
Row 3: K1, *k3, yo, CDD (see Glossary), yo, k3; rep from * to last st, k1.
Row 5: K1, *k1, yo, ssk, k3, k2tog, yo, k1; rep from * to last st, k1.
Row 7: K1, *k2, yo, ssk, k1, k2tog, yo, k2; rep from * to last st, k1.

For more abbreviations, stitches, and techniques, see Glossary.

INSTRUCTIONS (MAKE 2)

With larger needle and A, cast on 45 sts.
Work in K1, P1 Rib for 18 rows (approximately 3"/7.5cm). Join B and work as follows: *With A and B held together, work in K1, P1 Rib for 2 rows. With A only, work in K1, P1 Rib for 2 rows; rep from * 6 more times. Cut B. Continue with A.

Change to smaller needle and decrease on next RS row as follows: *K4, k2tog; rep from * 6 more times, k3. 38 sts. Purl 1 row.
Work rows 1–8 of Witchy Lace 5 times. Purl 2 rows.
Increase on next RS row as follows: *K1, kf/b; rep from * to end. 57 sts. Purl 1 row.
Next row: K1, *kf/b, k1; rep from * to end. 85 sts. Purl 1 row.
Place markers on next RS row (for thumb finishing) as follows (see Knitting Wisdom): K10, ppm, knit to last 10 sts, ppm, k10.
Continue in Stockinette stitch for 16 rows (approximately 2"/12.5cm), end after a RS row. With larger needle and A and B held together, bind off knitwise on next WS row.

FINISHING

Seam glove from cast on to bind off. With darning needle and A, create a thumb space in the Stockinette
stitch ruffle section, starting at the marker and sewing
from the first increase row to the bind off (parallel to the
seamed edge). Remove markers. Darn ends. Steam or
block to measurements.

Witchy Lace Chart

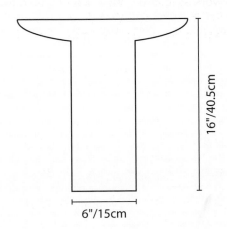

Witchy Lace Chart Key

☐ K on RS, P on WS

☑ K2tog

☑ SSK

☑ CDD (see Glossary)

☑ YO

☐ Repeat

16"/40.5cm

6"/15cm

Chapter 13

Invisible

She was only a niece, not a daughter, and therefore considered worthless. She was a hardworking girl, and in another family she would have been considered a treasure. Not here. She did what she could, knitting, sewing, making herself useful, but none of that mattered to her uncle, who spent good money on her food and board. He might have tossed her into the streets, but she was beautiful, which the uncle thought might be worth something one day.

That day finally came one autumn. She was told she was going to the market in the next town, but that was untrue, and if anything was to be sold, it was she. The cart kept on through the woods. The world was orange and gold and red. The niece was marveling over the great beauty of the countryside when all at once everything changed. A wall ringed a wicked land. There was dark magic here, and no birds flew in the trees; every woodland creature hid at the approach of the cart.

At last they came to a walled tower. The stones were the color of blood.

What is this place? she asked the driver.

Your husband's house, he said.

It was an arranged marriage. The uncle would have his gold and the husband would have his bride and she would have no say in the matter. She was taken into the tower over a path of stones that cried when you stepped on them. She lowered her eyes as she was introduced to her husband-to-be. He was very old, and his mouth turned down. He had already had three wives who had displeased him, but they were gone, and he looked pleased as punch when she came toward him. He appreciated her long black hair, her dark eyes, her youth. She insisted there had been a mistake; the situation was impossible, unthinkable. But no, she was the bride-to-be. He had the contract signed by her uncle in hand.

She was given a room where her wedding dress had already been hung in the closet and her wedding shoes were beside the bed. The dress was red and the shoes were crimson rather than white, and she could tell they had been worn by her predecessors. There were tears on the sleeves and blonde hairs on the collar, and on the soles of the shoes there was a thin layer of mud. She thought about escaping, but the windows were locked and the latch on the door would not be moved. When her dinner was brought up, she questioned the housemaid about her husband-to-be.

A terrible man, the housemaid said. *A hunter.*
What does he hunt? the niece asked.

The housemaid was old enough to be the girl's mother, and she had a kind heart. Out of pity she took the girl to a great hall. There were the pelts of bears and wolves. *He keeps them as pets; then, when he's bored, he skins them.*

In a cage, a fox was chained and starved.

The niece couldn't abide seeing a creature treated so.

Tell the man who is to be my husband I want the fox as my pet. In return, I will never say an unkind word to him.

The fox was brought to her room that evening. She signed a contract that she would never speak ill of her husband once they had married, then she took the fox from his cage and gave him milk and bread. He looked at her with dark eyes filled with gratitude. That night he slept at her feet.

The housemaid came to her the following morning. The older woman hadn't slept a wink all night. *There is one thing I haven't told you,* she confided. *He is a hunter of women as well. He has destroyed everyone who has ever been near him. What do you think happened to his other wives? They were married in red to hide the scars they would carry.*

Would no one defy him? the girl asked.

Where do you think the members of his family who opposed him are today? I am one of them. I am his sister, yet look what I have become.

The girl brooded then, and shed some tears. There was no way to run. She would be spied by the old man's watchmen if she tried to flee.

Not if you're invisible, the housemaid said.
How is that possible?

Impossible things are possible here. That is the danger of the place. But it may be your salvation.

The housemaid brought leaves from the trees in the woods and a pair of knitting needles. *No one will see you if you are a tree,* she said.

The wedding was the next day, so the niece knitted all through the night. When she was done she had made a hood the color of the elms and the oaks in the forest. The housemaid brought her to a secret door, but before she unlocked it, the housemaid wanted one promise: the niece must take the fox with her. She kissed the housemaid's cheek and promised she would. Then she and the fox went through the door.

It was the hour before light opened the sky. They went as quickly as they could, the fox leading the way through the twists and turns of the forest, across meadows and hills. When the sun at last began to rise, the niece slipped on the hood she had knitted, and in that instant she disappeared. She was invisible to the eyes of the guards who had been sent to find her. She might as well have been an elm or an oak, a stand of trees moving in the wind.

She might have lost her way a thousand times if it hadn't been for her companion. At last they came to the wall that kept the dark magic contained. The fox scrambled up and the niece followed, and once they were on the other side she took her hood off and the fox could see her as the woman she was, and she could see him as a handsome man, the nephew of the one who had once been her groom-to-be, who ruled a land that became nothing more than a memory as she and the housemaid's son walked hand in hand toward town.

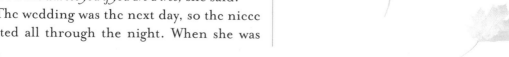

Invisible *Hood*

DIFFICULTY: Advanced beginner

MATERIALS

Noro Kureyon Air (109yd/100m, 3.5oz/100g) 100% Wool, 2 skeins in color #263 Tomato, Black, Brown. *Or any bulky-weight yarn that meets gauge.*

Approximately 1yd/1m of thinner yarn in matching color for seaming hem of hood.

Size 11 (8.0mm) needles or size to obtain gauge.

Additional needle for 3-needle bind off.

Darning needle.

One ⅝"/15mm button.

SIZES

One size (see Knitting Wisdom).

FINISHED MEASUREMENTS

19"/48cm circumference at neck, 28"/71cm circumference at top, 18¼"/46.5cm length.

GAUGE

9½ sts x 15 rows = 4"/10cm in Stockinette stitch, after blocking. *Take time to check your gauge.*

Knitting Wisdom

+ There is no need to work a buttonhole, as the stitches are big, and wool will stretch to allow a button through.

+ The pattern is written in one generous size. To make this smaller, maybe to fit a child or just to be a bit snugger, switch to a worsted-weight yarn. To make it even more generous and billowy, stay with a bulky yarn but use a larger needle for a looser gauge.

STITCH GUIDE

For abbreviations, stitches, and techniques, see Glossary.

INSTRUCTIONS

Cast on 80 sts.
Row 1 (RS): K2, *k1, p4; rep from * to last 3 sts, k3.
Row 2 (WS): K2, p1, *k4, p1; rep from * to last 2 sts, k2.
Rep rows 1 and 2 once more.
Decrease on next RS row as follows: K2, *k1, p1, p2tog, p1; rep from * to last 3 sts, k3. 65 sts.

Next row (WS): K2, p1, *k3, p1; rep from * to last 2 sts, k2.
Next row (RS): K2, *k1, p3; rep from * to last 3 sts, k3.
Work next WS row even as established.
Decrease on next RS row as follows: K2, *k1, p1, p2tog; rep from * to last 3 sts, k3. 50 sts.
Next row (WS): K2, p1, *k2, p1; rep from * to last 2 sts, k2.
Next row (RS): K2, *k1, p2; rep from * to last 3 sts, k3.
Work even for 3 more rows.
Decrease on next RS row as follows: K2, *k1, p2tog; rep from * to last 3 sts, k3. 35 sts.
Next row (WS): K2, p1, *k1, p1; rep from * to last 2 sts, k2.

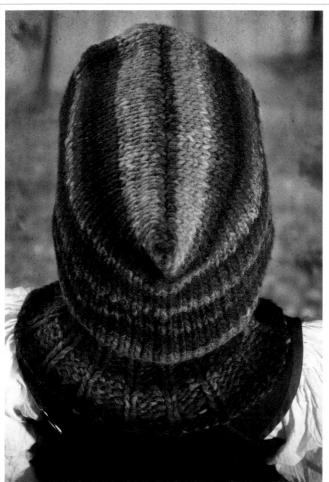

Next row (RS): K2, *k1, p1; rep from * to last 3 sts, k3. Work even for 3 more rows.

Increase on next RS row as follows: K2, M1, *k3, M1; rep from * to last 3 sts, k3. 46 sts.

Next row (WS): K2, purl to last 2 sts, k2.

Next row (RS): Knit.

Work next WS row even as established.

Begin front hood increases on next RS row as follows: K2, yo, knit to last 2 sts, yo, k2. 2 sts increased.

Next row (WS): K2, purl to last 2 sts, k2.

Rep last 2 rows 9 more times. 66 sts.

Work even, maintaining 2 st garter edges, for 24 rows.

FINISHING

Divide sts evenly in half onto 2 needles and fold hood with RS together. Join top of hood with 3-needle bind off. Darn ends. Where hood frames face, fold garter edge to inside and, using thinner yarn and darning needle, sew hem, starting from first yarn over increase row at left side and ending at first yarn over increase row on right side. Sew button to right side, just above collar on garter edge.

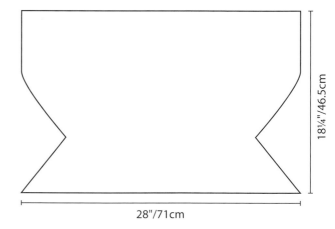

18¼"/46.5cm

28"/71cm

Chapter 14

Thorn

er baby was asleep in the cradle when there was a knock on the door. It was late, and the night was dark, and the dog growled.

But the knocking went on. It just wouldn't stop. It echoed down the hall. The mother didn't want the baby to wake, so she answered the door. She knew as soon as she did it that it was a mistake. The wind was cold, the leaves were piled up at the door, and there wasn't a star in the sky.

A woman had come to call, one the baby's mother had never seen before. She introduced herself as a new neighbor. Would it be possible for her to visit and have a cup of tea? Nothing fancy, but with a bit of sugar and milk? It was late, too late for visitors, but snow had begun to fall, and the kindhearted mother invited her guest in even though the room had grown colder in her presence. The stranger wore a black cape and her hair was held up with a silver pin in the shape of a branch of thorns. She looked young at first, but if you gazed at her through narrowed eyes she appeared to be old. She was so grateful to be taken in. She was lost, she said, and needed to get her bearings. Still the dog growled low in his throat, the way he did when there were wolves nearby.

The baby was asleep in her cradle. She was beautiful and sweet, a treasure her mother was grateful for each and every day. Most visitors cooed and rejoiced over the baby's charms, but the visitor said nothing. She didn't even glance in the baby's direction. She didn't have

to. She had been watching her through the windows for days.

The dog had begun to bark and needed to be tied up. The mother offered a comfortable chair to her guest, then she went to put the kettle on. In the time it took to do that and return with two cups of tea, the baby was gone. The dog stood in the doorway and howled. He pulled until he broke his leash so he could run across the snowy field. The mother chased after the dog in a panic. He tracked the baby to a house far away, on the other side of the woods, in a place so dark no one ever went there. It was surrounded by thorns, impassable. The mother did her best to get through, but her hands were cut to pieces and she was forced to back away weeping.

She ran to the house of her sisters, the dog at her heels. They heard her story, then told her what she must do. She must take the thorn trees and grind them into powder that must be added to a pot of dye that was the color of roses. She was then to knit and dye a blanket, one they vowed would always protect her child.

The mother did as she was told. When she was done, and the blanket was completed, she ran until she reached the edge of the woods filled with thorn trees. It was still impassable. The mother called to a crow to take the blanket to her baby, but how could a bird wrap a child in its wings? She called to a rabbit that darted under the thorns, but how could a rabbit whisper to her child not to cry? As she stood there, a soldier rode by, dressed all in metal. He was done with wars and was looking for a different sort of life, so he stopped and went to the young mother and asked how he might offer his help.

She told him her story and handed him the blanket, made of thorns and roses and her own tears. At that moment he realized he had found the life he wanted. He left the horse behind and made his way into the forest. It was dark and darker still. The thorns hit against his armor. Each time this happened he heard a ping that meant go back, but he went forward instead. Soon he came to a clearing in which there was a house made of black stones, surrounded by black rosebushes that had no flowers, only thorns. He looked in the window and spied the baby in a cradle and a very old woman, older than the thorn trees. She was asleep when he came through the door, so without a word he picked up the baby and wrapped her in the blanket that would ensure she would never come to harm.

When he brought the baby out of the forest, the look on her mother's face made him fall in love with her. At night the child dreamed of the day when she'd been found, when she was placed in her mother's arms as the tangle of thorns disappeared in a cloud of black smoke. She slept with the blanket until she had a child of her own, and then every night she wrapped up her own daughter, making certain she was always protected from harm.

Thorn *Blanket*

DIFFICULTY: Intermediate

MATERIALS

Cascade Yarns 220 Superwash (220yd/200m, 100g/3.5oz) 100% Superwash Wool, 8 skeins in color #902 Soft Pink.
Or any worsted-weight yarn that meets gauge (see Knitting Wisdom).

Size 8 (5.0mm) 32"/80cm needles or size to obtain gauge.

Stitch markers.

Darning needle.

SIZES

One size (see Knitting Wisdom).

FINISHED MEASUREMENTS

39"/99cm width, 41"/104cm length.

GAUGE

22 sts x 28 rows = 4"/10cm in Thorn Blanket stitch, after blocking.
Take time to check your gauge.

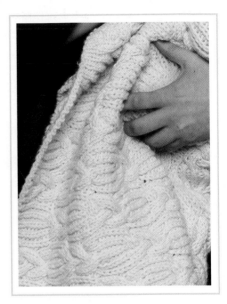

Knitting Wisdom

- ✦ Place markers for 2 garter selvedge stitches on each side of row 1 of edge ribbing.

- ✦ Place pattern repeat markers after edge ribbing on set-up row, then slip markers in all following rows.

- ✦ Blanket cast on is 2 selvedge stitches + multiple of 20 + 9 + 2 selvedge stitches. To resize blanket, add or remove stitches in multiples of 20.

- ✦ A smaller version of this blanket is shown in Pale Aqua. I used String Breeze, a cotton/silk/cashmere blend, for this version and cast on 153 stitches for a finished blanket measuring 28"/71cm × 33"/84cm.

- ✦ For baby blankets, refer to yarn label for washing instructions. I suggest washing before gifting. Use a lingerie bag and wash on gentle cycle to keep the blanket from stretching out of shape. Run in dryer until damp, then lay flat to dry if fiber allows or roll in towel first to eliminate moisture, then lay flat to dry. Include the lingerie bag and a note with easy washing instructions with the gift.

STITCH GUIDE

3/3 LC (3 Over 3 Left Cross)
Slip 3 sts to cable needle and hold to front, k3, k3 from cable needle.

3/3 RC (3 Over 3 Right Cross)
Slip 3 sts to cable needle and hold to back, k3, k3 from cable needle.

For more stitches, abbreviations, and techniques, see Glossary.

INSTRUCTIONS

Cast on 213 sts. Work edge ribbing as follows:
Row 1 (RS): K2, place selv marker, *[k1, p1; rep from * to last 3 sts, k1, place selv marker, k2.
Row 2 (WS): K2, sm, *p1, k1; rep from * to last 3 sts, p1, sm, k2.
Row 3: Rep row 1.
Row 4: Rep row 2.
Row 5: Rep row 1.

Set up for Thorn Blanket stitch on next WS row as follows: K2, sm, [p1, k1] 4 times, p1, *pm, k1, p9, pm, [k1, p1] 5 times; rep from * 9 more times, sm, k2.

Change to Thorn Blanket stitch, working Thorn Blanket Chart between selv markers, or follow written pattern as follows:
Row 1 (RS): K2, *[k1b (see Glossary), p1] 5 times, k3, 3/3 RC, p1; rep from * 9 more times, [k1b, p1] 4 times, k1b, k2.

Rows 2, 4, 6, 8, 10, and 12 (WS): K2, [p1, k1] 4 times, p1, *k1, p9, [k1, p1] 5 times; rep from * 9 more times, k2.
Row 3: K2, *[k1b, p1] 5 times, k9, p1; rep from * 9 more times, [k1b, p1] 4 times, k1b, k2.
Row 5: K2, *[k1b, p1] 5 times, 3/3 LC, k3, p1; rep from * 9 more times, [k1b, p1] 4 times, k1b, k2.
Row 7: Rep row 3.
Row 9: Rep row 1.
Row 11: Rep row 3.
Row 13: Rep row 5.
Row 14: K2, p9, [k1, p9] 20 times, k2.
Row 15: K2, *k3, 3/3 RC, p1, [k1b, p1] 5 times; rep from * 9 more times, k3, 3/3 RC, k2.
Rows 16, 18, 20, 22, 24, and 26: K2, p9, *[k1, p1] 5 times, k1, p9; rep from * 9 more times, k2.
Row 17: K2, *k9, p1, [k1b, p1] 5 times; rep from * 9 more times, k11.
Row 19: K2, *3/3 LC, k3, p1, [k1b, p1] 5 times; rep from * 9 more times, 3/3 LC, k5.
Row 21: Rep row 17.
Row 23: Rep row 15.
Row 25: Rep row 17.
Row 27: Rep row 19.
Row 28: K2, p9, [k1, p9] 20 times, k2.

Rep rows 1–28 of Thorn Blanket stitch 8 more times. Work rows 1–27 of Thorn Blanket stitch once more.

Change to edge ribbing and remove markers on next WS row:
Row 1 (WS): K2, *p1, k1; rep from * to last 3 sts, p1, k2.
Row 2 (RS): K2, *k1, p1; rep from * to last 3 sts, k3.
Row 3: Rep row 1.
Row 4: Rep row 2.
Row 5: Rep row 1.
Bind off in pattern on next RS row.

FINISHING

Darn ends. Wash blanket gently before gifting or using (see Knitting Wisdom).

Thorn Blanket Chart

Rows 14 and 28 are highlighted as a reminder that they are different from previous WS rows.

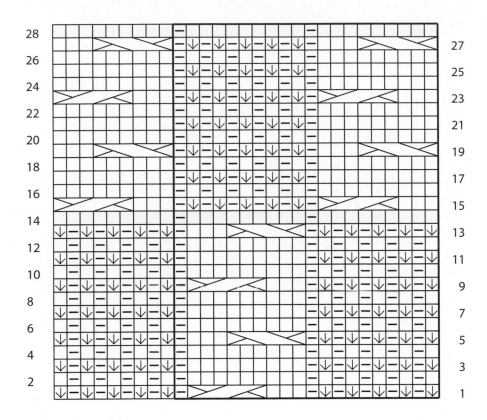

Thorn Blanket Chart Key

☐ K on RS, P on WS

⊟ P on RS, K on WS

↓ K1b

3/3 RC

3/3 LC

☐ Repeat

☐ Highlight

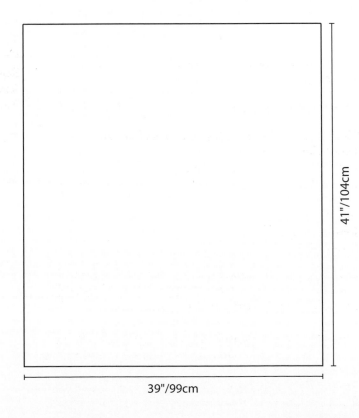

41"/104cm

39"/99cm

GLOSSARY

ABBREVIATIONS

1/1 LC: 1 over 1 left cross.

1/1 LPC: 1 over 1 left purl cross.

1/1 RC: 1 over 1 right cross.

1/1 RPC: 1 over 1 right purl cross.

3/3 LC: 3 over 3 left cross.

3/3 RC: 3 over 3 right cross.

BOR: Beginning of round.

CDD: Centered double decrease.

Dpn(s): Double-point needle(s).

K: Knit.

K1b: Knit 1 into the stitch below.

K1tbl: Knit 1 through the back loop.

K2tog: Knit 2 stitches together.

K3tog: Knit 3 stitches together.

Kf/b: Knit front/tback.

KYOK: Knit, yarn over, knit into same stitch.

M1: Make 1 stitch.

M1L: Make 1 left.

M1R: Make 1 right.

P: Purl.

P2tog: Purl 2 stitches together.

Pm: Place a marker.

Ppm: Place a permanent marker.

Psso: Pass slipped stitch over.

Rem: Remain(ing).

Rep: Repeat.

RS: Right side.

S1: Slip 1 stitch purlwise.

Selv: Selvedge.

Sm: Slip marker.

Ssk: Slip, slip, knit.

St(s): Stitch(es).

WS: Wrong side.

Wyib: With yarn in back.

Wyif: With yarn in front.

Yo: Yarn over.

TECHNIQUES

Cast Ons and Bind Offs

Thumb cast on

Wrap working yarn around left thumb from front to back. Insert right needle into the loop just created by wrapping yarn.

Lace bind off

Knit 1, *knit 1, pass first stitch over second stitch, yarn over and hold yarn to back, pass stitch over yarn over; repeat from * to end.

3-needle bind off

With the right sides of the two pieces together and the needles parallel, insert a third needle into the first stitch on each needle and knit them together. Knit the next 2 stitches the same way. Slip the first stitch on the third needle over the second stitch and off the needle. Repeat for 3-needle bind off.

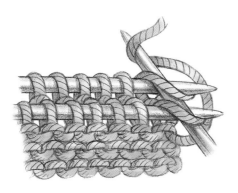

Increases

Knit, yo, knit (KYOK)

Make 3 stitches from 1 by knitting into front of next stitch (Figure 1), do not drop stitch off left needle (Figure 2), yarn over right needle (Figure 3), knit into front of same stitch again, drop stitch from left needle (Figure 4).

Figure 2

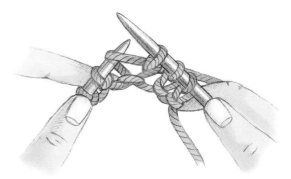

Figure 3

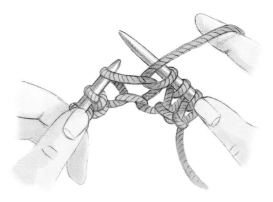

Figure 4

Figure 1

Kf/b

Increase 1 stitch by knitting into the front and back of the next stitch.

M1

Make 1 stitch by lifting the bar between 2 stitches with left needle from front to back (Figure 1) and knitting this lifted stitch through the back loop to create a twisted stitch (Figure 2).

Figure 1

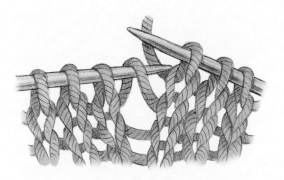

Figure 2

M1L

See M1.

M1R

Make 1 stitch leaning right by lifting the bar between 2 stitches with left needle from back to front (Figure 1) and knitting this lifted stitch through the front loop to create a twisted stitch (Figure 2).

Figure 1

Figure 2

Decreases

Centered double decrease (CDD)

Slip 2 stitches together knitwise to right needle, knit 1, pass 2 slipped stitches over the knit stitch.

K2tog
Knit 2 stitches together.

K3tog
Knit 3 stitches together.

P2tog
Purl 2 stitches together.

Ssk
Slip 1 stitch as if to knit, slip next stitch as if to knit, knit these 2 stitches together through back loops.

General Techniques

I-cord
With dpn, cast on 3 stitches. Knit 3. *Slide stitches to right end of your right needle (Figure 1), move needle to left hand without turning work, with yarn in back pull yarn from last stitch worked, knit 3 (Figure 2). Repeat from * to desired length. Bind off.

Figure 1

Figure 2

Knit 1 below (k1b)
Insert right needle into stitch 1 row below the next stitch on the left needle (Figure 1). Knit as normal, letting the stitch on your left needle drop (Figure 2).

Figure 1

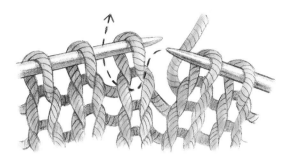

Figure 2

Kitchener stitch
Hold needle tips parallel, pointing in the same direction, wrong sides facing in. Set up stitches by threading tapestry needle through first stitch on closest (front) needle purlwise, leaving stitch on needle. Thread tapestry needle through first stitch on back needle knitwise, leaving stitch on needle. Repeat the following steps on the remaining stitches: Pull yarn through first stitch on front needle knitwise, letting stitch drop from needle (Figure 1). Pull yarn through first stitch on front needle purlwise, leaving stitch on needle (Figure 2). Pull yarn through first stitch on back needle purlwise, letting stitch drop from needle (Figure 3). Pull yarn through first stitch on back needle knitwise, leaving stitch on needle (Figure 4).

Figure 1

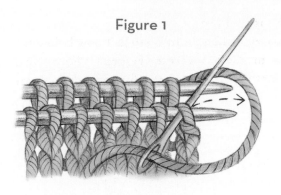

Figure 2

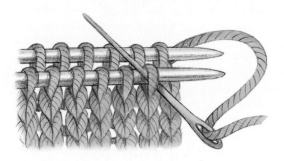

Figure 3

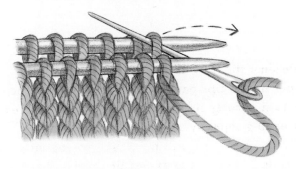

Figure 4

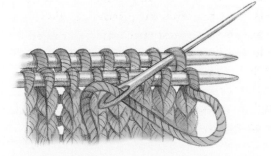

Pick up stitches knitwise

Insert needle from front to back into the center of the stitch closest to the edge; wrap the working yarn around the needle as if to knit; use the tip of the needle to pull that yarn through to the front of the fabric.

Pick up stitches purlwise

Insert needle from back to front into the center of the stitch closest to the edge; wrap the working yarn around the needle counterclockwise as if to purl; use the tip of the needle to pull that yarn through to the back of the fabric.

Place permanent marker (Ppm)

Place a permanent marker, which will stay in the same place until finishing, by hanging a split ring or locking stitch marker or by tying a strand of contrast yarn on the bar between the last stitch worked and the next stitch.

Faerie Knitting Notes

Make copies of this page for each of your faerie knits.

Project	
Start Date	Completed Date
Fiber	
Needle Size*	

*Always start with a gauge swatch to check your needle size, and measure your swatch to be sure it matches the pattern gauge.

Notes

_____

_____

_____

_____

_____

_____

_____

_____

_____

"Writing and knitting have a lot in common:
You have to have patience, imagination, and a willingness
to work on your mistakes. And of course, you have to
possess the desire to create something beautiful."

—ALICE HOFFMAN

US/Metric Conversion Charts

Length Conversions

To convert	to	multiply by
Inches	Centimeters	2.54
Centimeters	Inches	0.4
Feet	Centimeters	30.5
Centimeters	Feet	0.03
Yards	Meters	0.9
Meters	Yards	1.1

Knitting Needle Size Conversions

Metric Size	US Size
2mm	0
2.25mm	1
2.75mm	2
3mm	2.5
3.25mm	3
3.5mm	4
3.75mm	5
4mm	6
4.5mm	7
5mm	8
5.5mm	9
6mm	10
6.5mm	10
7mm	10.75
8mm	11
9mm	13
10mm	15
12.5mm	17
15mm	19
19mm	35
25mm	50

About the Authors

Alice Hoffman

Alice Hoffman is the *New York Times* bestselling author of more than thirty works of acclaimed fiction, including *The Rules of Magic*, *The Marriage of Opposites*, *Practical Magic*, the Oprah's Book Club selection *Here on Earth*, *The Museum of Extraordinary Things*, and *The Dovekeepers*. She has been in love with fairy tales since she began to read. Connect with Alice at AliceHoffman.com, on *Instagram* (@ahoffmanwriter), on *Twitter* (@ahoffmanwriter), or on *Facebook* (@AliceHoffmanAuthor).

Lisa Hoffman

Lisa Hoffman, knitwear designer and knitting teacher, lives in New York City with her husband, Andrew. She has three grown children living near and far. Lisa Hoffman's designs have been published in *Vogue Knitting*, *Interweave Knits*, and *knit.wear* magazines. She has projects published in books including Alice Hoffman's *Survival Lessons*, *Vogue Knitting: Mittens & Gloves*, Iris Schreier's One + One series, and *60 Quick Baby Blankets*, among others. She has original patterns for sale on her Ravelry.com site, *Lisa Hoffman Knitting*. She currently works and teaches knitting classes in New York City. Connect with Lisa at LisaHoffmanKnits.com, on *Instagram* (@directedknitting), or on *Facebook* (@lisahoffmanknits).

Share photos of your finished knits, see behind-the-scenes photos, and connect with Alice and Lisa at FaerieKnitting.com, on *Facebook* (@faerieknitting), at *Ravelry* (www.ravelry.com/patterns/sources/faerie-knitting/patterns), or on *Instagram* (@faerieknitting).